Polish

Learn Polish for Beginners: A Simple Guide that Will Help You on Your Language Learning Journey

Good luck & have fun learning
Patrycja

Contents

Introduction

Congratulations on making the life-changing decision to learn a foreign language. Knowing another language has recently become one of the most valuable skills to have, and not only in the job market. Due to the globalization and the fast development of technology, the whole world has become an interconnected web. Today, we work in multinational companies, take part in international webinars, and travel to the most beautiful places in the world. No one can imagine going abroad without knowing a tiny bit of English or the local language. Thus, the decision to learn a foreign language, especially an "exotic one", seems to be one of the best investments you can make. Plus, the investment can be made without huge sums of money—as long as you stick to affordable yet reliable and informative sources (like this book!).

Your decision to learn a foreign language is a bit more specific—as you decided to learn Polish. However, whatever your motivation for doing so, you won't be disappointed. Before you immerse yourself in learning, let's get familiarized with some basic information about both the country of Poland and the Polish language.

The country of Poland has existed since 966 AD—the year of declaring Christianity as a national religion by the first Polish king. Poland is located in Central Europe and shares its borders with

Germany on the west, the Czech Republic and Slovakia in the south and Ukraine, Belarus, Lithuania and a bit of Russia on the east. In the north, it has access to the Baltic Sea (around 400 km of the coastline).

Polish is certainly not one of the most spoken languages in the world—since it is the official language of Poland exclusively. It has around 38 million speakers in Poland, but many immigrants in countries such as the USA, UK, Germany, Norway, and Ireland are Polish. The Polish Community Abroad includes, for example, more than one million Poles in the UK and nearly one million in the States. What is also interesting is that many Americans are of Polish origin—due to the mass emigration caused by the difficult political situation in Poland in the 18th and 19th centuries.

Many native speakers of English consider Polish (along with Chinese, Arabic and Japanese) as one of the hardest languages to learn due to its heavy inflectional system and, probably, pronunciation. It may be partially true; however, the beginning is always the toughest part of any language journey, yet speaking one of the hardest languages in the world is quite an achievement.

Polish is a Slavic language, yet its written form is not based on the Cyrillic alphabet but the Latin script. Therefore, the Polish sounds can be tough to learn, especially some unusual consonant clusters like *szcz* or *dźdż*. However, the more you practice the pronunciation, the more automatic it becomes. Furthermore, the beginning is always the hardest part of any language journey since your first language data interferes with the new data that comes into your mind.

This book will teach you the vocabulary and grammar basics, along with some cultural background. With just fifteen-twenty minutes of practice a day, you will be able to have a decent conversation in the target language, and your use of Polish will improve.

Now let's take a look at some features of Polish that English speakers might find unusual and are not familiar with:

• The Polish language contains seven cases (nominative, genitive, dative, accusative, ablative, locative, and vocative). The cases might make the process of learning a little overwhelming at the beginning, but there's nothing to be afraid of.

• The Polish gender system is very different from the English one—since gender in Polish is grammatical, whereas it is biological in English. For instance, the Polish word *stół* [table] is masculine, *książka* [book] is feminine, and *jajko* [egg] is neutral.

• Polish is a highly inflectional language— it means that nouns, verbs and other parts of speech can have different endings or prefixes, depending on the case, gender, number, tense, and other features.

• Due to the abundance of inflections, Polish sentences can be created in multiple ways. Unlike English, Polish does not require a fixed order (such as subject + verb + object). Although there are more popular patterns, you can place each word in a sentence randomly, and it will be grammatically correct (of course, there are some minor exceptions).

• All Polish women's first names end with the vowel "a", except for the ones with foreign origin.

• Polish shares many grammatical and lexical features with the other Slavic languages, such as Czech or Slovak.

• Because of the influence of the inflectional system, Polish people add inflections to foreign names. For instance, you can notice different suffixes added to Harry Potter or Spiderman in different cases (like Harrego Pottera, Spidermana, Harremu Potterowi, Spidermanowi, etc.).

• There are only three grammatical tenses in Polish—past, future, and present. The rules of forming tenses are quite different too—since tenses are created by adding a suffix or a prefix in most cases.

• Polish people put a lot of stress on formal forms of address. It is highly advisable to address a person you don't know or your boss/teacher with a word *Pan/Pani* instead of just *you*. Addressing someone by using the *you* form in situations like a job interview or a formal meeting is considered rude.

Before getting into the actual learning, you need to know that this book is not a grammatical textbook. It is meant to teach you the basics of Polish to give you the foundations, and at the same time, make your learning fun, straightforward, easy, and enjoyable. Long and boring foreign language classes at school are probably things of the past—and you don't want to go back to the textbooks full of tough exercises and lists of words to memorize for a test. This book will provide you not only with the knowledge about the language but also with some cultural background based on real-life experiences.

The book consists of several chapters divided into subchapters that explain some grammatical rules, teach vocabulary, and provide you with some exercises based on repetition and using logical thinking and creativity. You can expect some exercises that will make you recall knowledge that you have already acquired while learning from the previous chapters. Thus, it is advisable to start from the beginning in order to make the most of the learning program included. Without further ado, let's get straight into the learning.

Good luck!

Chapter 1 – The Very Basics

To make the process of learning fast, fun and enjoyable, let's equip you with some general information about the Polish language—several basic rules of creating a sentence, some essential vocabulary, and a handful of useful expressions. Learning can run smoothly, provided that the process is ordered in some way. In other words, it is better to learn the basic units at the beginning, and then go to the advanced structures. Thus, let's introduce the Polish pronouns.

Pronouns

English appears to contain only a few personal pronouns when compared to Polish. Why? The answer is pretty simple: Polish personal pronouns are inflected by case, gender, and number. Think for a moment about the English personal pronouns. What are they? You probably know that there are only three ways of using an English pronoun; for example, *me*, *my* and *mine* or *you*, *your* and *yours*.

Polish pronouns are quite different since each pronoun has not three but seven different forms. Why? Each pronoun looks different in each case (as mentioned earlier, there are seven cases in the Polish language). Pronouns look different not only in different cases but also in different genders and numbers. For now, let's stop theoretical explanations and see how Polish pronouns work in practice. You are about to learn the basic Polish pronouns:

Ja – I

Ty – you

On – he

Ona – she

Ono – it

My – we

Wy – you

Oni/one – they

These pronouns are in the so-called nominative case. It means that they are in primary form. To be more precise, they are just equivalents of the English ones—they have the same meaning. Now, let's repeat the Polish pronouns. Try to focus on pronunciation.

Ja – I

Ty – you

On – he

Ona – she

Ono – it

My – we

Wy – you

Oni/one – they

You have probably noticed that the last pronoun, *they,* has two different forms in Polish. *Oni* is for masculine, and *one* is for the feminine. You can use *oni* when you refer to a group of men and *one* when you refer to a group of women. When the group consists of men and women, you always use *oni*. To sum up, *oni* is a more general pronoun—it can refer to a group of men or mixed groups—but *one* can refer only to a group of women.

Exercise: Try to guess the Polish pronouns based on the English equivalents:

I

You

He

She

It

We

You

They

Now let's try to do the same exercise once again but in a random order:

You

She

They

I

He

You

It

We

Congratulations! You have just learned the basic set of Polish pronouns. The last thing to remember is the distinction between the masculine and feminine pronoun *they*. It is vital to know the difference from the beginning—since the pronoun *they* is a classic example of interference between languages, so it can be harder to acquire.

Let's try another exercise:

How do you refer to the group of men?

How do you refer to the group of women?

How do you refer to the group of men and women?

Having learned the Polish pronouns, let's move on to the next step.

Być – to be

Knowing only some pronouns will not take you far. In order to make a first proper sentence, we need two ingredients—a subject (that can be a pronoun that you've already learned) and a verb. Thus, let's teach you one of the most important verbs: *być* [to be]. Before we start, let's brush up on the Polish pronouns. Try to guess the Polish pronoun based on the English one:

I

You

He

She

It

We

You

They

The Polish verb być [to be] will be a piece of cake. Let's see how it works:

Ja jestem – I am

Ty jesteś – you are

On jest – he is

Ona jest – she is

Ono jest – it is

My jesteśmy – we are

Wy jesteście – you are

Oni/one są – they are

The Polish verb *być* [to be] is not that irregular as the English one. It looks totally different in the last option—with the pronoun *oni/one* [they]. Although *być* is not that difficult, it requires some exercise to make itself comfortable in your mind. Let's repeat everything and try some exercises:

Ja jestem – I am

Ty jesteś – you are

On jest – he is

Ona jest – she is

Ono jest – it is

My jesteśmy – we are

Wy jesteście – you are

Oni/one są – they are

Exercise: Try to guess the verb *być* based on the English equivalents.

I am

you are

he is

she is

it is

we are

you are

Oni/one – są

Let's randomize the order a little:

You are

She is

They are

I am

He is

You are

It is

We are

Before we move on to the next level and try to add another ingredient to our sentence, let's explore something interesting. Polish verbs don't require the pronoun in a sentence. In other words, you don't have to say *ja jestem* [I am] to be fully understood. Instead, you can say *jestem* [I am], and it will be perfectly fine. You can omit the pronoun because the ending in *być* carries all the necessary information about the person or the doer of the activity. As mentioned, this rule applies to all Polish verbs, but now let's focus on *być*.

Let's see how the process works in practice:

jestem – I am

jesteś – you are

jest – he is

jest – she is

jest – it is

jesteśmy – we are

jesteście – you are

są – they are

Exercise: Try to guess the English equivalent based on the Polish form of *być*:

jestem

jesteś

jest

jest

jest

jesteśmy

jesteście

są

Congratulations! You have just learned the essential ingredient of the Polish language that will make your learning go smooth and easy. As promised, let's move on to the next level.

Formal pronouns

Before you are introduced to the formal pronouns, you need to know that formality and keeping the distance is a thing in Poland. Polish people use polite forms a lot in formal situations. For example, it is impossible to imagine a Polish student addressing their teacher using *ty* [you]. There is a general Polish rule that says, "If you don't know a person, it is advisable to use a formal form of address." Otherwise, your behavior might be considered rude. If you know a person, yet he/she is not a member of your family, a co-worker or a friend, use formal forms of address too. If you have known someone for a while in Poland, you can suggest *"przejście na ty"*, which literally means *"switching to you [form]"*.

So what are the formal pronouns that you should definitely know and use daily in Poland? Here they are:

You (singular) – Pan/Pani

You (plural) – Panowie/Panie/Państwo

Let's look at the distinction between feminine and masculine in the singular form of *you*. You can use *Pan* if you want to address a man, and *Pani* if you want to address a woman. Now, let's focus on the distinction in the plural form of *you*. You can use *Panowie* if you address a group of men, *Panie* when you address a group of women and *Państwo* when you address a mixed group or a couple (for example a married couple). To sum up, we have a set of formal forms of address, and they have their own distinctions based on gender. Since they are not only quite a mess but also absent in the English language, let's do some exercises.

Exercise: Try to come up with the correct answer.

How do you address one woman?

How do you address one man?

How do you address a group of men?

How do you address a married couple?

How do you address a group of women?

How do you address your teacher (female)?

How do you address your boss (male)?

How do you address an old lady?

How do you address your friend's parents?

How do you address a female shop assistant?

How do you address a policeman?

It was a demanding exercise since it required you to imagine a real situation, yet, as previously mentioned, a pronoun is not the whole story. We need at least a verb to produce something meaningful and functional. When we use the *you* form, we treat it as a second person singular or a second person plural. However, formal forms of address act like a third person singular. First, let's look at the *you* form (informal):

You are (singular) – ty jesteś

You are (plural) – wy jesteście

Now, let's focus on the formal forms of address. They look like this:

You are (singular) – Pan/Pani <u>jest</u>

You are (plural) – Panowie/Panie/Państwo <u>są</u>

To sum up, if you decide to use a formal form of address, you no longer use a verb that corresponds with a second person. Instead, you switch to a form of a third person. Since this phenomenon is quite challenging, let's do some exercises.

Exercise: Try to guess the Polish forms of address and their corresponding *to be* verb based on the English equivalents and the context provided. Remember that you have to switch to the third person in Polish! Take your time, and don't get discouraged. This is a tough exercise since it is based on an element that doesn't exist in English. Try to imagine the situation.

You are – a woman

You are – a group of men

You are – a married couple

You are – a man

You are – your boss (male)

You are – your teacher (female)

You are – an old man

You are – your friend's parents

You are – a policeman

You are – a waitress

You are – two men

You are – two women

It was a hard exercise! Now, you have gained more opportunities just by learning a handful of very basic language items. Let's take you a level higher!

Questions

It is time to ask some questions using the newly acquired verb *być* [to be]. As far as English is concerned, a question is formed in the process of inversion. You just make a subject (for example a pronoun) and a verb switch their places, and that's it. In Polish, a question can be formed in various ways. The first way of forming a question is based on using a special word *czy*—something that acts like the English *do* in questions, such as *do you like*? etc. Let's look at the examples:

Am I? – Czy (ja) jestem?

Are you? – Czy (ty) jesteś?

Is he? – Czy (on) jest?

Is she? – Czy (ona) jest?

Is it? – Czy (ono) jest?

Are we? – Czy (my) jesteśmy?

Are you? – Czy (wy) jesteście?

Are they? – Czy (oni/one) są?

So the Polish pattern is as follows. Firstly, we have to say *czy*, then we say a person (a pronoun in this case), and at the end, we say the verb *być*. The good news is that the form of *być* remains unchanged in questions. What is more, saying a person is totally optional– sometimes it is better to avoid mentioning a subject since it may sound unnatural. Let's try some exercises. For the exercise you are about to do, let's use the pronoun in questions.

Exercise: Try to build a question using *czy*, *być*, and a pronoun based on the English questions.

Am I? –

Are you? –

Is he? –

Is she? –

Is it? –

Are we? –

Are you? –

Are they? –

Now, let's randomize the order a little.

Are we? –

Am I? –

Is he? –

Are they? –

Is she? –

Are you? –

Is it? –

Are you? –

Remember what was previously mentioned about the questions at the beginning? There are different ways of forming a question in Polish. The second way doesn't require using the special word *czy* that acts like an interrogative word. It requires only the verb and nothing else, yet if you want to use this form, you have to change your intonation. When asking a question with only a verb, you must use rising intonation. Let's see the examples to make everything clear:

Am I? – jestem?

Are you? – jesteś?

Is he? – jest?

Is she? – jest?

Is it? – jest?

Are we? – jesteśmy?

Are you? – jesteście?

Are they? – są?

Now you are familiar with the most common way of asking questions in spoken Polish. Yes, Polish people usually don't use the first way when they speak. To make a conversation smooth and efficient, they prefer the second way based on changing the intonation. It is time you practiced your intonation too.

Exercise: Try to form a question using a rising intonation based on the English equivalents.

Am I? –

Are you? –

Is he? –

Is she? –

Is it? –

Are we? –

Are you? –

Are they? –

Let's try in a random order:

Are we? –

Am I? –

Is he? –

Are they? –

Is she? –

Are you? –

Is it? –

Are you? –

You have just learned how to ask a question in Polish. However, remember that most of the time, you will be faced with strangers; thus, it is advisable to ask a question with some formal forms of address. Remember that the formal forms switch from the second person to the third person. Here you can use only the first way—the one with the special interrogative word *czy*. Let's analyze the examples:

Are you (singular)? – Czy Pan/Pan jest?

Are you (plural)? – Czy Panowie/Panie/Państwo są?

It is time to practice the formal ways of asking a question. Again, imagine a situation and choose one suitable option. Focus on proper pronunciation.

Exercise: Try to form formal questions based on the English equivalents and the context provided. Remember that you have to switch to the third person in Polish!

Are you? – a woman that you've just met in a park

Are you? – a man that is sitting next to you on a train

Are you? – a female shop assistant

Are you? – your friend's parents

Are you? – your host family

Are you? – your IT teacher

Are you? – your boss

Are you? – a woman that works in a tourist information center

Are you? – a doctor

Are you? – two men that are talking

Are you? – two women that you are talking with

Are you? – a couple that you are talking with

With some essential vocabulary that you are going to learn in the following chapters, you will be confident enough to get creative with the questions you have learned here. Let's go to another level!

Negatives

Stop for a moment and summarize what you have already learned. If you've got to this stage, you probably know Polish pronouns with their formal equivalents, the most important verb—*być* [to be]—and how to ask a question. Congratulations! Let's take you to another step—expressing negatives in Polish. To learn how to create negative forms of *być*, let's go back to the positive forms. Try to do this quick and easy introductory exercise.

Exercise: Try to guess the Polish form *być* based on the English equivalents. If you are confident enough, you don't have to use pronouns.

I am –

You are –

He is –

She is –

It is –

We are –

You are –

They are –

This quick exercise should have shown you how easy the process of forming negatives is. If you want to create a negative form, you just add the word *nie* to the verb, and that is it! Polish *nie* means *no* and is used also as a negative word in a sentence. Let's look at some examples.

TIP: Remember that the pronoun is optional.

I am not – (ja) nie jestem

You aren't – (ty) nie jesteś

He isn't – (on) nie jest

She isn't – (ona) nie jest

It isn't – (ono) nie jest

We aren't – (my) nie jesteśmy

You aren't – (wy) nie jesteście

They aren't – (oni) nie są

Now it is time to practice a little. Let's do some quick and easy exercises.

Exercise: Try to guess negative forms of *być* (you should be confident enough to do it in a randomized order now):

You aren't –

She isn't –

They aren't –

I am not –

You aren't –

It isn't –

He isn't –

We aren't –

Before we move on to the next level, let's explore how to express negatives with formal pronouns. Remember what was previously mentioned at the beginning about the formal forms of address and their form? They act like a third person, not the second person. Let's take a look at some formal pronouns accompanied by a negative form of *być*:

You (singular) aren't – Pan/Pani nie <u>jest</u>

You (plural) aren't – Panowie/Panie/Państwo nie są

To sum up, formal forms of address in negative expressions are based on the same rule—you just add the word *nie* before the verb. Nevertheless, you have to remember that it is no longer the second person singular. Let's try a short exercise.

Exercise: Try to come up with 'formal negatives' based on the English equivalents and the context provided:

You aren't – a male shop assistant

You aren't – a couple you've just met on the train

You aren't – a woman that is sitting next to you on the bus

You aren't – a group of people that have just come to your company to see your boss

You aren't – your boss (female)

Well done! You know Polish pronouns, one of the most essential verbs and formal forms of address that you will be using a lot in Poland. Before we move on to some real context, let's look at some challenging exercises that summarize everything you have acquired.

A short Revision

Exercise 1: Try to form Polish expressions based on the English equivalents. You can use long or short forms.

She is –

It isn't –

Are they? –

He isn't –

I am –

Are you? –

They aren't –

You are –

She isn't –

We aren't –

It is –

I am not –

Are they? –

We are –

He is –

Is it? –

Exercise 2: Based on what you have learned in this chapter, try to guess whether the person requires a formal form of address.

Your close friend that you've known a lifetime

Your new boss

Your friend's parents you're seeing for the first time

Your parents

Your teacher

A shop assistant

Your brother

A stranger that you want to ask for directions

Your grandma

A policeman

A waiter

Your boyfriend/girlfriend

Exercise 3: Try to use the Polish *pronoun* + *to be* expression based on the English equivalents and the context provided. It is your task to decide whether a particular person requires a formal form of address. Take your time and focus on the task as this requires using your imagination!

You are – Your close friend that you've known a lifetime

Are you? – Your new boss

You aren't – Your friend's parents you're seeing for the first time

Are you? – Your parents

You aren't – Your teacher

You are – A shop assistant

Are you? – Your brother

You aren't – A stranger that you want to ask for directions

You are – Your grandma

Are you? – A policeman

You are – A waiter

You aren't – Your boyfriend/girlfriend

Now let's go up another level!

Introducing Oneself

As you go through the learning in this book, do all the exercises, and focus on each task, you will notice some positive effects. Think for a moment about all the stuff that you have already learned and take your time.

Now it is time to teach you how to introduce yourself and begin a simple conversation. We won't be covering detailed questions and answers—as you will learn more in the other chapters. For now, let's just see how you can say your name.

The most common pattern of introducing yourself in Polish is as follows: You say, "*Jestem* [I am]" and add your name. You have already learned the verb *być* [to be], so introducing yourself won't be a problem.

Exercise: Try to introduce yourself in Polish.

The second way of introducing yourself is saying, "*Mam na imię*" and adding your name. *Mam na imię* can be translated as *My name is*.

Exercise: Try to introduce yourself in Polish using *mam na imię*.

You can, of course, say your full name—your first name + last name. To do that, you cannot use *mam na imię*; you have to use *nazywam się* and add your name.

Exercise: Try to introduce yourself in Polish using *nazywam się*.

Now you have learned how to introduce yourself. When it comes to informal situations, use *jestem* or *mam na imię* phrases. It is better to use *nazywam się* and say your full name in formal situations.

Saying your name is a good start, yet it is better to know the question too. You need to understand at least that someone is asking you to introduce yourself! Actually, there are two ways of asking someone. You can use *jak masz na imię*? to know someone's first name or you can use *jak się nazywasz*? to know someone's full name.

When you hear *jak masz na imię*? you can say *jestem* + your name or *mam na imię* + your name. When you hear *jak się nazywasz*? you usually say *nazywam się* + your full name. Let's make these phrases work in practice.

Exercise: Try to answer in Polish these questions.

Jak masz na imię?

Jak się nazywasz?

Jak masz na imię?

Jak się nazywasz?

You can now introduce yourself in Polish or ask someone about his/her name! It is good to know that you don't have to use *jestem/mam na imię or nazywam się* all the time. You can just say your name or full name, and it will be fine! Sometimes it is even better to say only a name without a phrase because it makes your language use less artificial.

Let's summarize your conversation skills. Someone has just asked you to introduce yourself, and you successfully replied. What is the next step? You have to ask the person about his/her name. You can do it using the phrase *a ty?* which literally means *and you?* Let's try to do it!

Exercise: Try to introduce yourself and ask someone to introduce himself/herself.

We are not done with introductory questions. We need to learn some formal stuff that will be even more useful since it is Poland, remember? As previously mentioned, it is better to use *nazywam się* in a more serious conversation—since Polish people almost always say the full name in formal situations.

To ask someone to introduce himself/herself formally, you need to use patterns:

Jak się Pan/Pani nazywa? – What is your name?

Now imagine a situation and try to ask someone about his/her name. Let's provide some context, yet you will have to decide whether it is formal or not and use the most suitable way of asking this question.

Exercise: Try to ask about a person's name based on the provided context.

A new person in your class

Your father's friend from school

Your new teacher

Your new boss

A random person you've just met in a restaurant

A new member of your sports team

A new coworker

A policeman

Great! You are making your first steps towards having a decent conversation in Polish!

Chapter 2 – Numbers

Numbers in Polish may seem a little tricky at the beginning, but don't worry. We'll show you how to hack your way through this complex numeric system so that you will conclude that it wasn't as black as it was painted.

Numbers 0–10

Let's start with something fairly easy—how to count from 0 to 10. Your task is to say all the numbers out loud.

TIP: Focus on proper pronunciation.

zero – zero

one – jeden

two – dwa

three – trzy

four – cztery

five – pięć

six – sześć

seven – siedem

eight – osiem

nine – dziewięć

ten – dziesięć

Now, let's do that again, a little slower this time. Repeat all the numbers twice.

zero – zero, zero

one – jeden, jeden

two – dwa, dwa

three – trzy, trzy

four – cztery, cztery

five – pięć, pięć

six – sześć, sześć

seven – siedem, siedem

eight – osiem, osiem

nine – dziewięć, dziewięć

ten – dziesięć, dziesięć

TIP: The more times you say all the words out loud, the faster you will learn.

Next, try to repeat all the numbers one by one.

zero

zero, jeden

zero, jeden, dwa

zero, jeden, dwa, trzy

zero, jeden, dwa, trzy, cztery

zero, jeden, dwa, trzy, cztery, pięć

Stop here for a moment. Take a deep breath and repeat all those numbers once more. From 0 to 5.

zero, jeden, dwa, trzy, cztery, pięć

Let's continue counting.

zero, jeden, dwa, trzy, cztery, pięć, sześć

zero, jeden, dwa, trzy, cztery, pięć, sześć, siedem

zero, jeden, dwa, trzy, cztery, pięć, sześć, siedem, osiem

zero, jeden, dwa, trzy, cztery, pięć, sześć, siedem, osiem, dziewięć

zero, jeden, dwa, trzy, cztery, pięć, sześć, siedem, osiem, dziewięć, dziesięć

Repeat the numbers several times if you need to.

At this point, you may have noticed that Polish is full of hissing sounds—impossible to pronounce when you are a beginner. However, they represent the pure essence of this language. Okay, are you ready for some practice? Let's use the numbers!

Exercise 1: What is your telephone number? – Jaki jest Twój numer telefonu?

One of the primary uses of numbers from 0 to 10 is when you are talking about phone numbers.

In Poland, the format of a mobile phone number is nine digits divided into three parts. Therefore, when somebody asks a Polish person for their phone number, they usually reply with three 3-digit numbers, e.g., 609-345-812 (six hundred and nine, three hundred and forty-five, eight hundred and twelve).

For this practice, we'll show you the easy way, which is also commonly used in Poland. When you learn bigger numbers, we will go back to this subject again.

If you want to ask someone what their phone number is, you simply say:

Jaki jest Twój numer telefonu?

Take a moment to repeat this phrase several times.

Jaki jest Twój numer telefonu?

A person may reply:

Mój numer telefonu to…

Or simply start dictating their phone number.

Let's try it now. You shall be asked a question, and you will answer with *"mój numer telefonu to…"* and give your number:

Jaki jest Twój numer telefonu?
Mój numer telefonu to…

Let's do it again.

Jaki jest Twój numer telefonu?
Mój numer telefonu to…

Easy, isn't it? Do you want to spice it up a little? You shall be provided with three different phone numbers in English. You simply have to translate them into Polish:

509-432-611
812-790-665
608-419-723

Exercise 2 – Plus and minus – Plus i minus

We will continue our practice with some simple calculations. The purpose of this exercise is for your brain to be able to name random numbers without thinking about them too much. You want to skip the whole in-head translation, and this will definitely help.

Let's start with a couple of phrases.

When you want to ask how much a number *plus* another number is, you say:

Ile jest 2 plus 3? – How much is 2 plus 3?

To reply, you say:

2 plus 3 to jest 5. – 2 plus 3 is 5.

When you want to ask how much a number *minus* another number is, you say:

Ile jest 7 minus 1? – How much is 7 minus 1?

To reply, you say:

7 minus 1 to jest 6. – 7 minus 1 is 6.

Here are ten simple examples, and your task is to calculate the result and answer with a full sentence.

Ile jest 10 – 4?
Ile jest 1 + 1?
Ile jest 4 + 3?
Ile jest 9 – 6?
Ile jest 5 + 5?
Ile jest 4 – 2?
Ile jest 8 – 3?
Ile jest 1 + 8?
Ile jest 9 – 5?
Ile jest 2 + 6?

Feel free to practice more if you need to.

Next, you will learn the numbers from 11 to 20.

Numbers 11–20

It is about time to fill your number vocabulary with some "big fish"—expect even more hissing sounds.

eleven – jedenaście

twelve – dwanaście

thirteen – trzynaście

fourteen – czternaście

fifteen – piętnaście

sixteen – szesnaście

seventeen – siedemnaście

eighteen – osiemnaście

nineteen – dziewiętnaście

twenty – dwadzieścia

Have you noticed that all numbers from 11 to 19 end with *naście*? It means more or less *teen* in English. Makes sense, huh?

The majority of them are also constructed in a very simple way— that is a number from 1 to 9 + *naście*.

Now, repeat those numbers again, a little slower this time.

eleven – jedenaście

twelve – dwanaście

thirteen – trzynaście

fourteen – czternaście

fifteen – piętnaście

sixteen – szesnaście

seventeen – siedemnaście

eighteen – osiemnaście

nineteen – dziewiętnaście

twenty – dwadzieścia

How about you repeat all the numbers now from 0 to 20? Repeat all of them at least twice.

zero – zero

one – jeden

two – dwa

three – trzy

four – cztery

five – pięć

six – sześć

seven – siedem

eight – osiem

nine – dziewięć

ten – dziesięć

eleven – jedenaście

twelve – dwanaście

thirteen – trzynaście

fourteen – czternaście

fifteen – piętnaście

sixteen – szesnaście

seventeen – siedemnaście

eighteen – osiemnaście

nineteen – dziewiętnaście

twenty – dwadzieścia

Let's put it into practice now.

Exercise 1

This exercise is divided into two parts. In the first, you will be asked to translate the numbers into Polish. In the second, you will continue with simple calculations to keep your brain at top speed. Here we go!

Translate the following numbers into Polish:

seventeen

eleven

thirteen

twenty

eighteen

twelve

fifteen

nineteen

sixteen

fourteen

Finish the following sentences. Calculate the result.

10 + 9 to jest…

3 + 10 to jest…

20 – 3 to jest…

8 + 8 to jest…

19 – 7 to jest…

12 – 1 to jest…

15 + 5 to jest…

10 + 8 to jest…

18 – 4 to jest…

9 + 6 to jest…

Exercise 2

You are officially about to level up with some more complex sentence structures with the use of numbers.

A perfect example to practice is by learning how to talk about your address. Most people in Poland live in flats, not houses; therefore, you have to know how to address both the number of the building and the apartment. Let's say that this is your address:

Nowa Street 13, flat number 4, which should look like this: **ul. Nowa 13/4**

You can be asked the following question:

Jaki jest Twój adres? – What is your address?

You will reply:

ul. Nowa 13/4 (read 'ulica Nowa trzynaście przez cztery)

The '/' symbol is read as *przez* and separates the building number from the flat number.

Now how would you say *Sokola Street 2, flat number 11* in Polish?

If you said, "*Ul. Sokola 2 przez 11*," you're on fire! Let's practice more.

Woronicza Street 8, flat number 20
Spacerowa Street 5, flat number 1
Hoża Street 12, flat number 19

This is only to show you the correct format of an address in Poland, so next time you see it, you will be able to say it properly!

Big numbers (21-100)

So far, you have learned numbers from 0 to 20. Great job! The good news is… from this point it is going to be a little less complicated. All the donkey work is done, so you should enjoy this part. Let's start with some big guys… numbers from 21 to 100!

Don't worry; you won't have to repeat 100 numbers. Instead, you will be provided with some guidelines, and your job is to follow them to name the numbers yourself successfully. A little theory is crucial though.

Say these words out loud, one after another:

twenty – dwadzieścia

thirty – trzydzieści

forty – czterdzieści

fifty – pięćdziesiąt

sixty – sześćdziesiąt

seventy – siedemdziesiąt

eighty – osiemdziesiąt

ninety – dziewięćdziesiąt

one hundred – sto

Similar to the numbers from 11 to 20, these have something in common. They all start with a single digit number (from 1 to 9) and have a particular ending. Now, most of them end with *dziesiąt*, which simply translates to *ty* as in *forty*. But… the first three numbers are quite different. Let's repeat them twice this time.

TIP: Remember that the ending changes from the number 50.

twenty – dwadzieścia, dwadzieścia

thirty – trzydzieści, trzydzieści

forty – czterdzieści, czterdzieści

fifty – pięćdziesiąt, pięćdziesiąt

sixty – sześćdziesiąt, sześćdziesiąt

seventy – siedemdziesiąt, siedemdziesiąt

eighty – osiemdziesiąt, osiemdziesiąt

ninety – dziewięćdziesiąt, dziewięćdziesiąt

one hundred – sto, sto

Repeat all the numbers several times so that you can move on to the next challenge.

Once you have learned all of the above, you can practically name every single number from 0 to 100. Simply add a number from 1 to 9 at the end, and you are all set. Do you want to try? Here are a couple of examples first.

Repeat:

Twenty-three – dwadzieścia trzy

Thirty-nine – trzydzieści dziewięć

Sixty-six – sześćdziesiąt sześć

Eighty-two – osiemdziesiąt dwa

Are you getting the idea of how easy it is? Now, you try. Here are ten examples in English, and your task is to translate them into Polish. Ready? Let's begin!

78

51

60

100

83

47

62

34

29

95

How about we use these numbers and learn something useful at the same time? It is time for some more exercises.

Exercise 1 – Ile masz lat? – How old are you?

You are going to learn how to ask somebody their age, and how to reply.

There is a significant difference when it comes to talking about your age in English and Polish. In Polish, we say, "*I have x year'*," not "*I am x years old.*"

The word for *I have* is *mam* (and it has nothing to do with a mother). You also need a word for *years*, which is *lat*. So, how would you say *I am 31 years old* in Polish?

Mam trzydzieści jeden lat.

Here are a couple more examples before things get complicated. Your task is to translate the following sentences into Polish:

I am 25 years old.
I am 68 years old.
I am 41 years old.
I am 15 years old.
I am 9 years old.

Now, let's add a little complication to this. You are already familiar with the fact that Polish words like to change their endings depending on several factors. Same goes for 'years' in Polish. In most cases, you are going to use *lat* as in the examples above. But… this word has two other forms, *lata* and *rok*. Let's start with the latter.

We use *rok* in one case only, when something is 1 year old. That person might say:

"Mam rok."

Let's skip the fact that a one-year-old person wouldn't be able to talk about their age, so use your imagination here. Now, repeat it, "*Mam rok.*" Repeat it as many times as you want until it is stuck in your head.

Let's move on to *lata*. There are only three cases in which you will use this ending. When a number (no matter how big) ends with 2, 3 or 4, you will use *lata*, e.g.:

Mam dwa lata.
Mam pięćdziesiąt trzy lata.
Mam dwadzieścia cztery lata.

There are three exceptions. If you want to say that you are 12, 13, or 14 years old, you will use *lat*, not *lata* (even though these numbers end with 2, 3, and 4). So let's practice these numbers only. Say these sentences out loud:

Mam dwanaście lat.
Mam trzynaście lat.
Mam czternaście lat.

Let's sum up all the information so that you are not confused. Repeat all the phrases.

We use *rok* only if we want to say:

I am one year old. – Mam rok.

We use *lata* with numbers that end with 2, 3 or 4 (except 12, 13 and 14), e.g.:

I am 4 years old. – Mam cztery lata.
I am 32 years old. – Mam trzydzieści dwa lata.
I am 63 years old. – Mam sześćdziesiąt trzy lata.

We use *lat* with all the other numbers, e.g.:

I am 5 years old. – Mam pięć lat.
I am 12 years old. – Mam dwanaście lat.
I am 48 years old. – Mam czterdzieści osiem lat.
I am 91 years old. – Mam dziewięćdziesiąt jeden lat.
I am 70 years old. – Mam siedemdziesiąt lat.

Okay, let's practice. You will be asked to translate the English sentences into Polish, keeping in mind the correct form of the word 'years'. But first, here is one more thing to learn. If you want to ask someone their age, you will say:

"Ile masz lat?"

Say it several times, and let's start the exercise.

Ile masz lat? (45)
Ile masz lat? (12)
Ile masz lat? (1)
Ile masz lat? (99)
Ile masz lat? (62)
Ile masz lat? (24)
Ile masz lat? (100)
Ile masz lat? (38)
Ile masz lat? (13)
Ile masz lat? (53)

Exercise 2 – Ile to kosztuje? – How much is it?

Now let's learn how to use numbers when asking for a price. The currency in Poland is called *złoty*. You should know that the word *złoty* changes too. We'll explain it to you, but you may find it a lot easier as you have already learned different forms of *years* in the previous exercise. Here, the rule is pretty much the same. Let's have a look.

Złoty can have three different endings and everything depends on the last digit of the number we are using it with. Therefore, there is:

złoty

złote

złotych

We use *złoty* with only one number in Polish, which is *jeden*. So, if anything costs 1 zł, you are going to say:

jeden złoty

Easy. Now repeat *jeden złoty* several times.

We use *złote* with numbers *dwa, trzy, cztery* and all the other numbers where the last digit is '2', '3' or '4' except '12', '13', and '14'. So, we can say that something costs:

siedemdziesiąt dwa złote

dwadzieścia trzy złote

pięćdziesiąt cztery złote

The only exceptions are the three numbers mentioned above (12, 13, and 14). All the other numbers, no matter how big they are, will go with *złote*—as long as they end with *dwa, trzy* or *cztery*. Now let's practice a little. Here are several examples and you simply add either *złoty* or *złote*:

sześćdziesiąt trzy…

trzydzieści dwa…
jeden…
osiemdziesiąt cztery…
trzy…

The last form is *złotych,* and you will use it with all the other numbers. Here are some examples. Say them out loud, one after another:

pięć złotych
dziesięć złotych
dwadzieścia osiem złotych
pięćdziesiąt jeden złotych
sto złotych

You should understand how the word changes now, but just in case you are still a little confused, let's sum it up.

We use *złoty* when we are talking about something that only costs '1 zł'; therefore, you say:

To kosztuje jeden złoty.

One more time. *To kosztuje jeden złoty* means *It costs 1 zł.* Say it several times *To kosztuje jeden złoty.*

Let's move on.

We use *złote* with numbers that end with 2, 3 or 4 (except 12, 13 and 14). How would you say *It costs 42 zł*?

To kosztuje czterdzieści dwa złote.

And *It costs 24 zł*?

To kosztuje dwadzieścia cztery złote.

Perfect. One more case to go.

We use *złotych* with all the remaining numbers. How would you say *It costs 12 zł*?

To kosztuje dwanaście złotych.

And *It costs 95 zł?*

To kosztuje dziewięćdziesiąt pięć złotych.

Let's do some serious exercises now.

Exercise 3

In this exercise, you will answer one question. In each case, you will have to use the correct form of the word *złoty*. Feel free to repeat the question out loud too. You will need it when communicating in Polish. Ready? Let's begin.

Ile to kosztuje? (3 zł)
Ile to kosztuje? (45 zł)
Ile to kosztuje? (12 zł)
Ile to kosztuje? (100 zł)
Ile to kosztuje? (62 zł)
Ile to kosztuje? (1 zł)
Ile to kosztuje? (23 zł)
Ile to kosztuje? (89 zł)
Ile to kosztuje? (51 zł)
Ile to kosztuje? (34 zł)

Ordinal numbers

You may be wondering why you need to learn ordinal numbers too. Well, you will need them to be able to talk about time. Before we get into more detail, you have to know the difference between the Polish way of measuring time and the American one.

In Poland, people use a 24-hour clock, which means that the words *am* and *pm* don't exist. If you want to say it is 1 pm, you will actually have to say *it's 13 o'clock*. Let's have a quick look at the Polish time format. From 1 am till noon, there is no difference; therefore, we have:

1 am – 1

2 am – 2

3 am – 3

4 am – 4

5 am – 5

6 am – 6

7 am – 7

8 am – 8

9 am – 9

10 am – 10

11 am – 11

12 am – 12

Easy, isn't it? Now, here is where the big difference is present:

1 pm – 13

2 pm – 14

3 pm – 15

4 pm – 16

5 pm – 17

6 pm – 18

7 pm – 19

8 pm – 20

9 pm – 21

10 pm – 22

11 pm – 23

12 pm – 24 or 00

Converting into the 24-hour format is fairly easy—you just have to add 12 to each hour after the clock strikes noon. But that is not even the point here. Our goal is to learn how to talk about time, so here it goes.

Ordinal numbers are crucial if you want to be able to talk about time. For this lesson, we will only focus on the first 24 numbers and the feminine form. Oh, and all adjectives change depending on the gender of the noun. Here, the word *hour*, in Polish *godzina,* has a feminine form; therefore, you will have to use a feminine form of the adjective that appears before it.

If you want to ask someone what time it is, you will say:

"Która jest godzina?"

To answer, you will simply start with:

"Jest…"

And you will add the time.

Let's start with ordinal numbers. Try to say all the words out loud and repeat them as many times as you need.

It's 1 am. – Jest pierwsza.
It's 2 am. – Jest druga.
It's 3 am. – Jest trzecia.
It's 4 am. – Jest czwarta.
It's 5 am. – Jest piąta.
It's 6 am. – Jest szósta.
It's 7 am. – Jest siódma.
It's 8 am. – Jest ósma.
It's 9 am. – Jest dziewiąta.
It's 10 am. – Jest dziesiąta.

It may be a little too much; therefore, repeat all the numbers again.

pierwsza
pierwsza, druga
pierwsza, druga, trzecia
pierwsza, druga, trzecia, czwarta
pierwsza, druga, trzecia, czwarta, piąta

pierwsza, druga, trzecia, czwarta, piąta, szósta

pierwsza, druga, trzecia, czwarta, piąta, szósta, siódma

pierwsza, druga, trzecia, czwarta, piąta, szósta, siódma, ósma

pierwsza, druga, trzecia, czwarta, piąta, szósta, siódma, ósma, dziewiąta

pierwsza, druga, trzecia, czwarta, piąta, szósta, siódma, ósma, dziewiąta, dziesiąta

Feel free to revise all of them until you have memorized the first batch of ordinal numbers. Once you have learned them and are comfortable, move on to the next part: ordinal numbers from 11 to 24.

One more time, how do you say *What's the time?* in Polish? If you said *Która jest godzina?* you can be proud of yourself. We haven't mentioned that question for a while now, so good job if you still remembered it.

All right, say all the sentences out loud:

It's 1 pm. – Jest trzynasta.

It's 2 pm. – Jest czternasta.

It's 3 pm. – Jest piętnasta.

It's 4 pm. – Jest szesnasta.

It's 5 pm. – Jest siedemnasta.

It's 6 pm. – Jest osiemnasta.

It's 7 pm. – Jest dziewiętnasta.

It's 8 pm. – Jest dwudziesta.

It's 9 pm. – Jest dwudziesta pierwsza.

It's 10 pm. – Jest dwudziesta druga.

It's 11 pm. – Jest dwudziesta trzecia.

It's 12 pm. – Jest dwudziesta czwarta.

The last four hours are pretty easy as you only add the digits you have already learned. Now, let's repeat the above numbers once again, but slower:

trzynasta

trzynasta, czternasta

trzynasta, czternasta, piętnasta

rzynasta, czternasta, piętnasta, szesnasta

trzynasta, czternasta, piętnasta, szesnasta, siedemnasta

trzynasta, czternasta, piętnasta, szesnasta, siedemnasta, osiemnasta

trzynasta, czternasta, piętnasta, szesnasta, siedemnasta, osiemnasta, dziewiętnasta

trzynasta, czternasta, piętnasta, szesnasta, siedemnasta, osiemnasta, dziewiętnasta, dwudziesta

trzynasta, czternasta, piętnasta, szesnasta, siedemnasta, osiemnasta, dziewiętnasta, dwudziesta, dwudziesta pierwsza

trzynasta, czternasta, piętnasta, szesnasta, siedemnasta, osiemnasta, dziewiętnasta, dwudziesta, dwudziesta pierwsza, dwudziesta druga

trzynasta, czternasta, piętnasta, szesnasta, siedemnasta, osiemnasta, dziewiętnasta, dwudziesta, dwudziesta pierwsza, dwudziesta druga, dwudziesta trzecia

trzynasta, czternasta, piętnasta, szesnasta, siedemnasta, osiemnasta, dziewiętnasta, dwudziesta, dwudziesta pierwsza, dwudziesta druga, dwudziesta trzecia, dwudziesta czwarta

Now, instead of repeating all the numbers one by one, let's mix them up. You will have to say what the time is based on the given example in English:

Która jest godzina?
(It's 2 am.)
Która jest godzina?
(It's 6 am.)
Która jest godzina?
(It's 12 am.)
Która jest godzina?
(It's 9 pm.)
Która jest godzina?
(It's 12 pm.)
Która jest godzina?
(It's 4 pm.)

Of course, we can go on and on, but that is not the point. Why? Because we have only learned round hours. To be able to talk about time, you will have to know how to say minutes as well. We will show you the easiest way possible so that you literally don't have to memorize anything new.

As previously mentioned, to talk about the time you have to know ordinal numbers. You should, however, be aware of one crucial thing: you will use them only to name the first part of the time, i.e., when referring to hours. For the second part—minutes—you will use regular numbers, which you already know. Here is an example:

If you want to say that *It's 10:15 am*, you simply say

Jest dziesiąta piętnaście.

See? The first part (hour) is an ordinal number, while the second one (minutes) is a regular number. No philosophy here. Here are some more examples. Let's start with an English version and give you time to think of the Polish equivalent. Make sure you say them out loud as many times as you need:

It's 2:15 pm. – Jest czternasta piętnaście.
It's 1:20 pm. – Jest trzynasta dwadzieścia.
It's 5:30 am. – Jest piąta trzydzieści.
It's 4 pm. – Jest szesnasta.
It's 9:30 pm. – Jest dwudziesta pierwsza trzydzieści.
It's 9:15 am. – Jest dziewiąta piętnaście.
It's 2:24 am. – Jest druga dwadzieścia cztery.
It's 8:25 pm. – Jest dwudziesta dwadzieścia pięć.
It's 1:05 pm. – Jest trzynasta pięć.
It's 3:30 am. – Jest trzecia trzydzieści.
It's 11:35 pm. – Jest dwudziesta trzecia trzydzieści pięć.
It's 5:40 pm. – Jest siedemnasta czterdzieści.
It's 6 am. – Jest szósta.
It's 8:45 am. – Jest ósma czterdzieści pięć.
It's 7:40 pm. – Jest dziewiętnasta czterdzieści.
It's 8:10 pm. – Jest dwudziesta dziesięć.

Exercise 1 – What's the time? – Która jest godzina?

This short exercise is your follow-up. Its main goal is to give you some extra practice so that you can revise what you have learned. In the first part, you are going to name ten different hours based on English examples. In the second part, you are going to do the opposite thing: you will be given ten various hours in Polish, and your task will be to change them into English versions, using *am* or *pm*. Ready?

Part 1 – Give Polish equivalents:
It's 10:12 am.
It's 5:16 pm.
It's 11:05 am.
It's 6:20 pm.
It's 12:55 pm.
It's 7:29 am.
It's 1:03 am.
It's 9:17 pm.
It's 11:10 am.
It's 4:40 pm.

Part 2 – Give the English equivalents:

Jest pierwsza czternaście.

Jest dziesiąta czterdzieści pięć.

Jest dwunasta osiem.

Jest dwudziesta pięćdziesiąt.

Jest osiemnasta trzydzieści.

Jest czternasta dziesięć.

Jest druga trzydzieści siedem.

Jest piąta pięć.

Jest dziewiętnasta dwadzieścia.

Jest dwudziesta trzecia pięćdziesiąt dziewięć.

Excellent! You have learned how to say how old you are, your telephone number, and other useful things.

Chapter 3 – Deconstructing Polish

Before we move on to the next level, let's summarize what you have already learned:

- how to conjugate a pronoun

- how to use "to be"

- how to introduce yourself

- how to address someone formally

- how to say how old you are

- how to count up to 100

- how to say your address

- how to use the Polish currency

- how to tell the time

Every time you forget about something you learned in a previous chapter, go back and check it. You don't need to hurry—this book doesn't require any deadline. Sometimes you might forget some rules, vocabulary, or expressions, and it is totally fine! Yet, without systemicity and constant repetition, you might get lost very quickly.

In this chapter, we are going to explain some rules of Polish grammar. Don't get discouraged—the whole process will be fun and interesting. If you want to proceed with learning Polish, you need to know why the words are ordered in a certain way in a sentence, and why some words have some strange endings.

Polish Verbs

If you want to learn Polish verbs successfully, you need to ditch English concepts that you already have in your mind. The first thing you need to know is that there are eleven different patterns of verb conjugation in Polish. Yes, eleven! And we are only talking about the present forms. If you want to learn them all by heart, don't do it—since it won't give you any good results. If you want to learn it, you need a strategy, so let's provide you with the best one!

In order not to get lost in the infinite amounts of conjugations and endings, we need to search for similarities and patterns. Essentially, nearly all Polish verbs in an infinitive form (the form without a person like *to be* in English) end with the letter [-ć]. What is more, each person has its own special ending added to the main part of the verb. Let's look at the verbs *robić* [to do], *czytać* [to read], and *śpiewać* [to sing]:

To do - robić

I do – ja robi**ę**

You do – ty robi**sz**

He does – on robi

She does – ona robi

It does – ono robi

We do – my robi**my**

You do – wy robi**cie**

They do – oni/one robi**ą**

To read – czytać

I read – ja czyta**m**

You read – ty czyta**sz**

He reads – on czyta

She reads – ona czyta

It reads – ono czyta

We read – my czyta**my**

You read – wy czyta**cie**

They read – oni/one czyta**ją**

To sing – śpiewać

I sing – ja śpiewa**m**

You sing – ty śpiewa**sz**

He sings – on śpiewa

She sings – ona śpiewa

It sings – ono śpiewa

We sing – my śpiewa**my**

You sing – wy śpiewa**cie**

They sing – oni/one śpiewa**ją**

Can you already see the pattern? Let's summarize. Despite some minor changes, the pattern remains the same:

- in the first person ja, there is always the ending [-m] or [-ę].

- in the second person ty, there is always the ending [-sz].

- in the third person on/ona/ono, there is nearly always no ending; you just delete [-ć] from the original infinitive form.

- In the first person plural, there is almost always the ending [-my].

- In the second person plural, there is almost always the ending [-cie].

- In the third person plural, there is always the ending [-ą].

The above pattern applies to *nearly* all verbs—since there are some exceptions. Yet you need to remember that some verbs undergo some minor changes like letter substitution or addition of a letter. These changes result from the fact that Polish people try to make the pronunciation a bit easier. For now, let's skip all the exceptions because the purpose of this chapter is to show you some patterns and teach you some necessary stuff. If you learn the pattern, you will be understood anyway, even though you might skip or wrongly substitute a letter. Now, let's try to remember the pattern by doing some exercises.

Exercise: Try to conjugate *grać* [to play]. Take your time and apply the endings analogically based on the examples shown.

TIP: The verb *grać* is similar to *czytać*.

To play – grać

I play –

You play –

He plays –

She plays –

It plays –

We play –

You play –

They play –

Here are the answers:

I play – ja gram

You play – ty grasz

He plays – on gra

She plays – ona gra

It plays – ono gra

We play – my gramy

You play – wy gracie

They play – oni/one grają

Exercise: Try to conjugate *dzwonić* [to call]. Take your time and apply the endings analogically based on the examples shown.

TIP: The verb *dzwonić* is similar to *robić*.

To call – dzwonić

I call –

You call –

He calls –

She calls –

It calls –

We call –

You call–

They call–

Here are the answers:

To call – dzwonić

I call – ja dzwonię

You call – ty dzwonisz

He calls – on dzwoni

She calls – ona dzwoni

It calls – ono dzwoni

We call – my dzwonimy

You call – wy dzwonicie

They call – oni/one dzwonią

Remember: the more you know about the language, the better. Before we move on to another step, congratulations You are making huge progress and gaining more and more confidence. It is vital to know the pattern since you are unable to learn all the different declensions by heart. Even if you somehow managed to learn them, you would hate learning Polish after a short period.

Reflexive Verbs

To learn Polish verbs successfully and use them with confidence daily, there is one more important thing you need to know—reflexive verbs. These verbs can be easily found in English—this is a group that requires using a special pronoun like *yourself/myself/themselves*. For example, *she washes herself, they watch themselves,* etc.

The good news is that the Polish group of these special reflexives is really easy to learn! Firstly, Polish reflexive verbs follow the same pattern and have more or less the same endings. One—and the only—thing you need to add to make a verb reflexive is the word *się*. *Się* acts like *myself/yourself/yourself/yourself/himself/themselves* in English and remains the same in each person. Let's look at some examples:

To wash oneself – myć się

I wash myself – ja myję się

You wash yourself – ty myjesz się

He washes himself – on myje się

She washes herself – ona myje się

It washes itself – ono myje się

We wash ourselves – my myjemy się

You wash yourselves – wy myjecie się

They wash themselves – oni/one myją się

To help oneself – częstować się

I help myself – ja częstuję się

You help yourself – ty częstujesz się

He helps himself – on częstuje się

She helps herself – ona częstuje się

It helps itself – ono częstuje się

We help ourselves – my częstujemy się

You help yourselves – wy częstujecie się

They help themselves – oni/one częstują się

See how easy it is? All you need to do is add *się* to the verb, and that is basically it! Now it is time to do some exercises.

TIP: You don't have to 'write a person' in Polish, as you probably remember from the first chapter. We suggest skipping pronouns—you should know them well anyway.

Exercise: Try to conjugate *kąpać się* (meaning similar to *myć się* [to wash oneself]). Don't get discouraged, even if you see some minor changes in spelling—the main idea of this exercise is to teach you some rules and patterns. As mentioned, it is impossible to memorize all the spelling patterns in different declensions by heart.

To wash oneself – kąpać się

I wash myself –

You wash yourself –

He washes himself –

She washes herself –

It washes itself –

We wash ourselves –

You wash yourselves –

They wash themselves –

Now, it's time to check the answers:

To wash oneself – kąpać się

I wash myself – kąpię się

You wash yourself – kąpiesz się

He washes himself – kąpie się

She washes herself – kąpie się

It washes itself – kąpie się

We wash ourselves – kąpiemy się

You wash yourselves – kąpiecie się

They wash themselves – kąpią się

Now you know why the word *się* is so popular in Polish and what it means. Before we move on to the next level, let's summarize all you need to know about verbs in Polish:

- Polish verbs have eleven different declensions that are closely related to the patterns of pronunciation.

- The essential part of each Polish verb is the ending—it carries information about the subject (gender/number/case).

- Each person has a different ending that remains the same in each declension. It's the most important pattern you need to learn.

- Polish reflexive verbs do not require different pronouns. All you need to do is add the word *się*. In fact, adding a pronoun is unnecessary since the ending in the verb carries all the necessary information.

Essential Polish Verbs That You Need To Know

It is time to leave grammar for a moment. Below is a list of the most important Polish verbs that might be useful. Unfortunately, there are no shortcuts—you need to learn them by heart. So stay in this chapter for a while and go through the list multiple times. The good news is that each verb contains a context—a sentence in which it might be used. You don't have to learn the sentences; focus on the verbs, and try to remember as many as possible. After you feel confident with the list, you can go straight to the quiz.

Być – to be (Jestem Paula – I am Paula)

Mieć – to have (Mam kota – I have a cat)

Iść – to go (Idę do sklepu – I'm going to the store)

Robić – to do/to make (Robię zakupy – I'm doing shopping)

Próbować – to try (Próbowałem wiele razy – I've tried many times)

Pomagać – to help (Pomagam tacie – I'm helping my dad)

Grać/bawić się – to play (Lubię bawić się na dworze – I like playing outside)

Spacerować – to walk (Lubisz spacerować? – Do you like walking?)

Uczyć się – to learn (W szkole muszę się uczyć – I have to learn at school)

Mieszkać – to live (Mieszkam w mieście – I live in a city.)

Pracować – to work (Pracuję w dużej firmie – I work in a big company)

Jeść – to eat (Chodźmy coś zjeść! – Let's go eat something!)

Pić – to drink (Ona wypiła już kawę – She has already drunk her coffee)

Pisać – to write (Piszę e-mail – I'm writing an e-mail)

Czytać – to read (On czyta książkę – He's reading a book)

Liczyć – to count (Mogę na ciebie liczyć? – Can I count on you?)

Rysować – to draw (Uczę się rysować – I'm learning how to draw)

Malować – to paint (Oni malują – They're painting)

Widzieć – to see (Nie widzę go – I can't see him)

Wyglądać/spoglądać – to look (Dobrze wyglądasz! – You look good!)

Oglądać – to watch (Oglądam telewizję – I'm watching TV)

Słyszeć – to hear (Usłyszałem dziwny głos – I've just heard a strange voice)

Słuchać – to listen (Słuchamy muzyki – We're listening to music)

Spać – to sleep (Idę spać – I'm going to sleep)

Gotować – to cook (Umiesz gotować? – Can you cook?)

Sprzątać – to clean (Muszę dzisiaj sprzątać mieszkanie – I have to clean the flat today)

Podróżować – to travel (Podrózuję do Chin – I'm traveling to China)

Jechać – to drive (Jadę do domu – I'm driving home)

Latać – to fly (Chciałbyś polecieć do Londynu? – Would you like to fly to London?)

Pływać – to swim (Nie umiem pływać – I can't swim)

Biegać – to run (Ona teraz biega – She's running now)

Siedzieć – to sit (Usiądźcie – Sit down)

Rozpoczynać – to begin (Przedstawienie zaczyna się o 8:00 – The show begins at 8 am)

Stać – to stand (Stań tutaj – Stand here)

Kłaść – to put (Gdzie mogę położyć tę paczkę? – Where can I put this parcel?)

Wychodzić – to leave (Właśnie wychodziliśmy – We were just leaving)

Przychodzić – to come (Przyjdź do mojego biura o 9:00 – Come to my office at 9 am)

Śpiewać – to sing (Nie umiem śpiewać – I can't sing)

Tańczyć – to dance (Zatańczymy? – Shall we dance?)

Pamiętać – to remember (Pamiętaj o mnie – Remember about me)

Zapominać – to forget (Zapomniałem o spotkaniu! – I've just forgotten about the meeting!)

Wybierać – to choose (Wybierz jedną opcję – Choose one option)

Zamykać – to close (Zamknij drzwi, proszę – Close the door, please)

Otwierać – to open (Czy mógłbyś otworzyć okno? – Could you open the window?)

Tworzyć – to create (Stwórzmy własny projekt! – Let's create our own project!)

Budować – to build (On buduje dom – He's building a house)

Pokazywać/przedstawiać – to show (Pokażesz mi? – Can you show me?)

Czuć – to feel (Czuję się dobrze – I feel good)

Czuć/wąchać – to smell (Czuję coś dziwnego – I'm smelling something strange)

Smakować/próbować – to taste (Spróbuj tej zupy – Taste this soup)

Myśleć – to think (Myślę, że... – I think that...)

Rosnąć – to grow (Dzieci rosną bardzo szybko – Children grow very fast)

Myć – to wash (Muszę umyć samochód – I need to wash my car)

Wierzyć – to believe (Wierzę, że… – I believe that…)

Mówić – to speak (Mów głośniej! – Speak up!)

Powiedzieć – to say (Powiedz coś! – Say something!)

Rozmawiać – to talk (Możemy teraz porozmawiać? – Can we talk now?)

Dawać – to give (Czy mógłbyś mi to dać? – Could you give me this?)

Brać – to take (Muszę wziąć dzień wolnego – I have to take a day off)

Pożyczać – to borrow (Pożyczysz mi swój samochód? – Could you borrow me your car?)

Pożyczać – to lend (Pożyczę ci mój samochód – I will lend you my car)

Skakać – to jump (On skacze bardzo wysoko – He's jumping very high)

Odejść – to quit (Odchodzę! – I quit!)

Uderzyć – to hit (Mocno mnie uderzyła! – She hit me hard!)

Strzelać – to shoot (Strzelaj! – Shoot!)

Kupować – to buy (Chcę kupić nowy samochód – I want to buy a new car)

Sprzedawać – to sell (Muszę sprzedać dom – I have to sell my house)

Wymieniać – to exchange (Czy mogę wymienić pieniądze? – Can I exchange my money?)

Wygrywać – to win (Moja drużyna wygrała zawody! – My team won the competition!)

Przegrywać – to lose (Moja drużyna przegrała zawody – My team lost the competition)

Rozumieć – to understand (Rozumiesz? – Do you understand?)

Uczyć – to teach (Uczę w szkole podstawowej – I teach at primary school)

Łapać – to catch (Łap piłkę! – Catch the ball!)

You have now learned most of (or even all) the verbs from the list. What is more, you can apply all the rules and patterns from the beginning of this chapter and make your verbs more meaningful. However, now it is time to have a short quiz and check how many verbs you know by heart.

Exercise: Write a Polish verb based on the English equivalents.

To read –

To do –

To buy –

To sell –

To learn –

To borrow –

To win –

To talk –

To watch –

To choose –

To open –

To build –

To swim –

To write –

To exchange –

To show –

To smell –

To run –

To give –

To take –

To jump –

To dance –

To leave –

To put –

To understand –

To hit –

To shoot –

To sit –

To begin –

To create –

Good job! You are confident enough to express your actions in Polish. These verbs will be really useful. In fact, sometimes it is better to say only a verb than to say nothing. A Polish person might eventually understand your intentions just by hearing one essential word. After all, communicative effectiveness is the key. Let's go to the next level.

Nouns – How Do They Work?

So you have just learned over 100 essential Polish verbs and the rules that apply to them as well. It is high time you were shown another essential ingredient of a sentence—the noun. We won't be teaching you any nouns in this chapter; instead, you will learn the rules based on which nouns are governed.

Cases:

As mentioned at the beginning of this book, seven different cases apply not only to nouns but also to adjectives. Before being too hard on yourself, please note that using a wrong case does not significantly affect communication. Although mastering the rules can be worthwhile, aiming at perfection can be daunting, especially at the beginning of your journey. Remember that if you apply a wrong suffix, your message will be ninety-nine percent understandable. Let's take a closer look at the words *książka* [book] and *komputer* [computer], to get familiar with the concept of Polish cases:

Nominative – książ_ka_

Genitive – książ_ki_

Dative – ksią_żce_

Accusative – książ_kę_

Ablative – (z) książ_ką_

Locative – (o) ksią_żce_

Vocative – książ_ko!_

Nominative – komput_er_

Genitive – komput_era_

Dative – komput_erowi_

Accusative – komput_er_

Ablative – komput_erem_

Locative – komput_erze_

Vocative – komput_erze_

As you can see, some of the endings look similar, yet no clear rules can be applied, as far as the suffixes are concerned. It is advisable to learn the cases gradually, in context, and by using associations. If you try to learn all variations of the same word by heart, you will find yourself overwhelmed sooner or later. So, don't worry.

Even some proper names need to be declined by case. Look at the examples below:

Francja [France] – feminine noun

Nominative – Francja

Genitive – Francji

Dative – Francji

Accusative – Francję

Ablative – (z) Francją

Locative – (o) Francji

Vocative – Francjo!

Włochy [Italy] – plural noun

Nominative – Włochy

Genitive – Włoch

Dative – Włochom

Accusative – Włochy

Ablative – (z) Włochami

Locative – (o) Włoszech

Vocative – Włochy!

Number:

As far as the grammatical number is concerned, Polish singular or plural are usually formed with different endings that correspond with gender. What is interesting in the Polish plural form is that there are only two genders—masculine and non-masculine. The usage of these endings is also not determined by any rules.

For example, the word *dom* [house] is masculine, yet it is an object. Then, its plural form, *domy* [houses], involves the ending –y. The word *mężczyzna* [man] is masculine and refers to a person. Its plural form *mężczyźni* [men] ends with –i.

Gender:

It was also mentioned at the beginning of the book that Polish masculine, feminine, or neuter do not correspond with the actual sex. The Polish language has grammatical gender, whereas English has biological gender. What is even more interesting is that Polish speakers use masculine or feminine often when talking about inanimate objects, such as pieces of furniture or fruits. For example, the Polish word *banan* [banana] is masculine, the word *truskawka* [strawberry] is feminine, and the word *mango* [mango] is neutral.

To sum up, the only way to learn different genders, numbers, and cases is by repetition and memorization. We don't want you to do some intimidating exercises involving gender, case, and number; we have just included some explanations to make you more aware of some essential differences between Polish and English. Now, equipped with the knowledge about the language, you can move on to some learning and practice in context!

Before we proceed to the next chapter, though, let's summarize what you have learned in this one:

- Polish verbs have eleven different declensions that are closely related to the patterns of pronunciation.

- The essential part of each Polish verb is the ending—it carries information about the subject (gender/number/case).

- Each person has a different ending that remains the same in each declension. It's the most important pattern you need to learn.

- Polish reflexive verbs do not require different pronouns. All you need to do is to add the word *się*. In fact, adding a pronoun is unnecessary since the ending in the verb carries all the necessary information

• Each Polish noun is declined by case, gender, and number. All the information about these three grammatical characteristics can be found in the ending of a particular noun.

• There are seven cases in Polish—nominative, genitive, dative, accusative, ablative, locative, and vocative.

• The Polish language has grammatical gender. It means that gender does not correspond with the actual sex. In fact, even an object can have a feminine or masculine gender.

• Polish plural has only two genders—masculine and non-masculine.

Chapter 4 – Greetings

In this chapter, you will learn some of the most important Polish greetings, including how to greet your friends, your boss, and even strangers on the street. Let's start with the basic daily greetings.

Polish everyday expressions are similar to the English ones with only one exception—Polish people do not use an equivalent of the English *good afternoon*. There is one expression in Polish that can be used in the morning and afternoon:

Dzień dobry! – Good morning/Good afternoon!

Let's repeat:

Dzień dobry! – Good morning/Good afternoon!

In the evening you need to say:

Dobry wieczór! – Good evening!

Let's repeat it twice:

Dobry wieczór! – Good evening!

Dobry wieczór! – Good evening!

If you want your expression to be really formal, you can add *Panie/Pani* + a name. This is how it works:

Dzień dobry Pani ... – Good morning Mrs./Ms. ...

Dzień dobry Panie ... – Good morning Mr. ...

Let's repeat. You can come up with a name and add it to the expression.

Dzień dobry Pani ... – Good morning Mrs./Ms. ...

Dzień dobry Panie ... – Good morning Mr. ...

The same rule applies to *good evening*. Let's see how it works:

Dobry wieczór Pani ... – Good evening Mrs./Ms. ...

Dobry wieczór Panie ... – Good evening Mr. ...

Let's repeat:

Dobry wieczór Pani ... – Good evening Mrs./Ms. ...

Dobry wieczór Panie ... – Good evening Mr. ...

If you want to greet your friend or a person that you have known for a while, you can use:

Cześć! – Hello/Hi!

It is important to know that the Polish *cześć!* is slightly different from the English *hello!/hi!* When you don't know someone, or you address a much older person, always use *dzień dobry* instead of *cześć*. When you are at work, it is advisable to say *dzień dobry/do widzenia (Pani/Panie)* instead of *cześć* (*cześć* is rather an informal form of address), unless you get to know your colleagues better. Also, students at school/university never say *cześć* to their teachers, and teachers do not use *cześć* when addressing to their students. If you want to address a teacher, always use *dzień dobry* and be polite, no matter how long you have known the teacher.

Now, let's repeat *cześć* at least three times since its pronunciation is quite hard:

Cześć! – Hello/Hi!

Cześć! – Hello/Hi!

Cześć! – Hello/Hi!

You can use *cześć* to say goodbye as well. It is quite a universal and multi-purpose word:

Cześć! – Bye!

Remember: *cześć* is an informal way of saying goodbye. If you want to say something formal, use:

Do widzenia! – Goodbye!

Let's repeat it twice:

Do widzenia! – Goodbye!

Do widzenia! – Goodbye!

If you want to make your goodbye even more formal, try the pattern with *Pan/Pani* + a name. Here is how it works:

Do widzenia Pani ... – Goodbye Mrs./Ms. ...

Do widzenia Panie ... – Goodbye Mr. ...

Let's repeat:

Do widzenia Pani ... – Goodbye Mrs./Ms. ...

Do widzenia Panie ... – Goodbye

After you greet someone, it is time to say *how do you do?/how are you?* etc. There are a couple of Polish phrases that you can use:

Co tam?/Co u ciebie? – How are you?/How do you do?

Let's repeat them twice:

Co tam?/Co u ciebie? – How are you?/How do you do?

Co tam?/Co u ciebie? – How are you?/How do you do?

It is important to note that expressions such as *how are you/how do you do* are perceived differently in Poland. If you ask a Polish person *how do you do?*, don't expect something like *I'm fine/I'm okay/I'm doing great*. Instead, a Polish person will tell you a couple of things about their job/school/family life, etc. So, the Polish *co tam/co u ciebie?* is slightly different from the English *how are you?*

It is time to practice a bit!

Exercise: How do you...

... greet your friend?

... say goodbye to your boss?

... say goodbye to your friend's parents?

... greet your Polish teacher in the morning?

... greet a stranger on the street in the evening?

... say goodbye to a shop assistant?

... greet your teacher in the afternoon?

... greet your new business partner in the evening?

... ask your Polish friend how does he or she do?

There are also some colloquial expressions that are mostly used by younger generations. It is good to know a couple of informal greetings as well, so let's take a look at some of them:

Siema! – Hey!

Elo! – Yo! (a very informal form of addressing your close friends)

Jak leci? – What's up?

Trzymaj się! – Take care!

Na razie! – Bye!

Dzięki! – Thanks!

Spoko!/Ok!/Okej! – Okay!/No problem! (Polish people say *okay* very often)

Let's repeat all the colloquial expressions:

Siema! – Hey!

Elo! – Yo!

Jak leci? – What's up?

Trzymaj się! – Take care!

Na razie! – Bye!

Dzięki! – Thanks!

Spoko!/Ok!/Okej! – Okay!/No problem!

Excellent! You have basically learned all of the useful expressions that you need to know to greet someone or say goodbye. Now it is time to start a real conversation. Let's move back to the first chapter for a while.

Remember how to introduce yourself? Take your time and try to say the phrases out loud…

Remember how to ask someone to introduce himself/herself? Again, take your time and pronounce the phrases…

Remember how to ask someone to introduce himself/herself formally? Think for a moment and pronounce the phrases…

Hopefully, you remember all the useful conversational phrases from the first chapter. The following is a complex exercise, but it will make you focus and wrap things up.

Exercise: Some context is provided based on what you will need regarding the Polish expressions that you have learned so far. This time, there aren't any English equivalents—it is your job to imagine a particular situation and choose an appropriate expression.

   1) You are meeting your new boss for the first time. Greet him/her and introduce yourself.

2) You are meeting your close friend from Poland. Greet him/her and ask how does he/she do.

3) You are meeting your new business partner (you've invited him/her for lunch). Greet him/her, introduce yourself, and ask him/her to introduce himself/herself.

4) You are in a supermarket. Greet the shop assistant.

5) You are meeting your new Polish teacher (your friend has just told you that he/she wants to see you in his/her office). Greet him/her and introduce yourself.

6) You are meeting a group of your very close friends. Greet them and ask how do they do.

7) Your friend invited a person you don't know to his birthday party (his cousin) Greet him/her, introduce yourself and ask how does he/she do.

8) The birthday party is over, and you decide to go home. Say goodbye to all of your friends.

9) A lunch with your business partner is over. Say goodbye to him/her.

10) You've just met your friend's mom on the street, and it's 10 pm. Greet her.

Good job! You are making huge steps towards fluency! If you are not confident enough with the previous chapters, go back and revise all the necessary phrases and vocabulary items. You will need them in each next chapter—make sure that you understand and remember most things. Let's move on to the next chapter, which is all about expanding your conversational limits.

Chapter 5 – An initial Conversation

Before we move on, let's go over some of the Polish skills that you have already learned. You can now:

- Greet someone, say hello/goodbye

- Greet someone formally using formal forms of address

- Introduce yourself

- Ask someone to introduce himself/herself

- Count to 100

- Tell the time

- Tell someone your phone number

- Ask about someone's address or tell them your address

- Use polish currency in multiple situations (e.g., while doing shopping)

As well as all the above skills, you have also learned some essential background knowledge about Polish grammar (pronouns, nouns, verbs). With all the skills and knowledge, you can now move on to more advanced Polish phrases!

How old are you?

Greeting someone and saying your name in a foreign language is a good start, yet it might be not enough. To actually have a simple conversation, you have to learn more phrases. Let's start by telling someone how old you are—you should go back to Chapter 2 and read the extract about age.

So how do you ask someone how old he/she is? Think for a second.

Ile masz lat?

Now say how old you are. If you don't remember how to express it, go back to Chapter 2. So, how can you say how old you are?

Mam... lat.

Remember that Polish people do not use the verb *być* [to be] while telling others their age. Instead, they use *mieć* [to have]. A literal translation would be *I have... years.*

Exercise: You already know Polish numbers. Try to say in Polish how old you are using different numbers.

I am 18 years old.

I am 54 years old.

I am 33 years old.

I am 97 years old.

I am 6 years old.

I am 45 years old.

I am 23 years old.

Now say your age.

Sometimes you will have to ask about someone's age politely. Here are the formal forms of the question *ile masz lat?*:

Ile ma Pan/Pani lat?

Ile mają Panie/Panowie/Państwo lat?

Let's repeat:

Ile ma Pan/Pani lat?

Ile mają Panie/Panowie/Państwo lat?

Good! Try to exercise a bit.

Exercise: Ask about someone's age politely based on the context provided.

A woman

A man

A group of women

A group of men

A group of men and women

Language

Questions about knowledge of a particular language are an inseparable part of nearly every foreign conversation. If you don't feel confident enough to handle a dialog, you can at least say that you don't know the language. Here are some essential phrases and questions that will definitely help you on your way. If you want to ask someone if he/she speaks a particular language, you need to say:

Mówisz po angielsku? – Do you speak English?

Mówisz po polsku? – Do you speak Polish?

And now let's look at the formal ways:

Czy mówi Pan po angielsku? (one male)

Czy mówi Pani po angielsku? (one female)

Czy mówią Panie po angielsku? (two or more females)

Czy mówią Panowie po angielsku? (two or more males)

Czy mówią Państwo po angielsku? (two or more males and females)

Czy mówi Pan po polsku? (one male)

Czy mówi Pani po polsku? (one female)

Czy mówią Panie po polsku? (two or more females)

Czy mówią Panowie po polsku? (two or more males)

Czy mówią Państwo po polsku? (two or more males and females)

It is advisable to use the formal forms, even though a person seems to be as old as you are. Remember: Polish people switch to the informal style after knowing someone for a while.

So, you can ask someone if he/she knows Polish/English. Now it is time to tell someone that you speak/don't speak Polish/English.

If you want to say that you **speak** Polish/English, you need to use:

Mówię po angielsku. – I speak English.

Mowię po polsku. – I speak Polish.

Let's repeat:

Mówię po angielsku. – I speak English.

Mowię po polsku. – I speak Polish.

If you want to say that you **don't speak** Polish/English, you need to use:

Nie mówię po angielsku. – I don't speak English.

Nie mówię po polsku. – I don't speak Polish.

If you want to say that you **don't speak** Polish/English **very well**, you need to use:

Nie mówię dobrze po angielsku. – I don't speak English very well.

Nie mówię dobrze po polsku. – I don't speak Polish very well.

That's a lot for the beginning. In order not to get lost, let's try some exercises.

Exercise: Try to say the following phrases in Polish.

Do you speak English? (informal way)

Do you speak Polish? (male, formal way)

Do you speak English? (female, formal way)

Do you speak Polish? (males, formal way)

Do you speak English? (females, formal way)

Do you speak Polish? (males and females, formal way)

I speak Polish.

I speak English.

I don't speak Polish.

I don't speak English.

I don't speak Polish very well.

I don't speak English very well.

Nationality and Place of Living

Another important part of an initial conversation is represented by asking about someone's address or nationality. Here we won't focus on telling the exact address—since you have already learned this skill in Chapter 2 (numbers). Instead, you will learn how to ask some basic questions about the country/nationality/city, etc.

Let's start with a broad context. If you want to ask someone about his/her nationality, you need to say:

Skąd pochodzisz? – Where are you from?

If you want to keep the polite style, you need to say:

Skąd Pan/Pani pochodzi?

Skąd Panowie/Panie/Państwo pochodzą?

If you want to tell someone where you are from, you need to say:

Pochodzę z... – I am from...

To add even more context, let's learn some vocabulary. You are about to learn some country names in Polish. Take your time and repeat all the names multiple times. As long as you get comfortable with the new piece of vocabulary, you can go further.

Countries – kraje:

Polska – Poland

Wielka Brytania – UK/Great Britain

Stany Zjednoczone/USA – the United States/the USA

Niemcy – Germany

Francja – France

Hiszpania – Spain

Czechy – the Czech Republic

Włochy – Italy

Portugalia – Portugal

Grecja – Greece

Holandia – the Netherlands

Belgia – Belgium

Węgry – Hungary

Słowacja – Slovakia

Ukraina – Ukraine

Turcja – Turkey

Dania – Denmark

Norwegia – Norway

Szwecja – Sweden

Finlandia – Finland

Chorwacja – Croatia

Irlandia – Ireland

Islandia - Iceland

Rosja – Russia

Chiny – China

Japonia – Japan

Australia – Australia

Brazylia – Brazil

Argentyna – Argentina

Kolumbia – Colombia

Meksyk – Mexico

Kanada – Canada

Egipt – Egypt

Izrael – Israel

Continents – kontynenty:

Ziemia – the Earth

Europa – Europe

Azja – Asia

Australia – Australia

Afryka – Africa

Antarktyda – Antarctica

Ameryka Północna – North America

Ameryka Południowa – South America

Ameryka Środkowa – Central America

Before we practice, there is one thing that you need to know. The Polish verb *pochodzić z* [to come from] makes the country appear in a different case (namely, the genitive case). So, if you want to say that you come from Europe, you can't use *Pochodzę z Europa*. Instead, you have to say *Pochodzę z Europy*. Here are more examples:

Pochodzę z Polski. – I come from Poland.

Pochodzę z Wielkiej Brytanii. – I come from Great Britain.

Pochodzę z Niemiec. – I come from Germany.

Pochodzę z Chin. – I come from China.

Pochodzę z Ukrainy. – I come from Ukraine.

Of course, all these cases are difficult to grasp at the beginning, so don't get discouraged. Even though you forget about using the genitive case, you will be understood anyway. Keep in mind that communicative effectiveness, not 100 percent accurate use, is the key. We have included some grammatical explanations to make your learning less ambiguous.

Let's practice.

Exercise: Try to say in Polish the following phrases.

I come from Poland.

I come from the USA.

I come from Great Britain.

I come from Germany.

I come from China.

I come from Belgium.

I come from Turkey.

I come from Ukraine.

I come from Sweden.

I come from Japan.

I come from Australia.

Excellent! You have learned some essential vocabulary and useful phrases connected to country/nationality. Now it is time to move to the narrow context. If you want to ask someone about his/her place of living, you need to say:

Gdzie mieszkasz? – Where do you live?

If you want to keep the polite style, you need to use the following phrases:

Gdzie Pan/Pani mieszka? – Where do you live? (one male/one female)

Gdzie Panie/Panowie/państwo mieszkają? – Where do you live? (females/males/males and females)

If you want to tell someone where you live, you need to use the following phrase:

Mieszkam w/na… (city/region etc.) – I live in…

Pretty easy, isn't it? To introduce more context, we will provide some useful vocabulary. You can use the new words to practice the *where do you live* phrase:

w Londynie – in London

w Nowym Jorku – in New York

w Warszaawie – in Warsaw

w Krakowie – in Cracow

w mieście – in a city

w dużym mieście – in a big city

w małym mieście – in a small town

na wsi – in the countryside

w domu – in a house

---

w bloku – in a block of flats

na północy kraju – in the north of the country

na południu kraju – in the south of the country

na wschodzie kraju – in the east of the country

na zachodzie kraju – in the west of the country

w pobliżu dużego miasta – near a big city

w centrum miasta – in the city center

na przedmieściach – in the suburbs

w górach – in the mountains

Try to go through the new set of vocabulary many times and try to remember as many new items as possible. There is no time pressure—you can always go back to the previous chapters if you want to make a short revision. If you are confident enough with the above list, you can practice a bit with the phrase.

Exercise: Try to say in Polish the following phrases.

Where do you live? (informal)

Where do you live? (formal, male)

Where do you live? (formal, female)

Where do you live? (formal, males)

Where do you live? (formal, females)

Where do you live? (formal, males and females)

I live in Warsaw.

I live in Cracow.

I live in a big city.

I live in the suburbs.

I live in the north of the country.

I live in the countryside.

I live in a house.

I live in a block of flats.

I live in the city center.

I live in the mountains.

I live near a big city.

Good job! You are making huge progress! You have learned many new vocabulary items and can incorporate these new items in a real context. Keep it up!

Useful Conversational Phrases

Sometimes a conversation doesn't go as planned. Even though you will have well-prepared scenarios in your head, most of the time, face-to-face interaction will always be surprising. You have to remember that every real dialog (not via SMS or any other instant messenger) requires improvisation. Thus, we have prepared a list of useful phrases that might be helpful during the initial foreign conversation you will take part in.

Some of the phrases that you are about to learn have already been introduced in the previous chapter, yet in a slightly different context. Go through the following list multiple times and repeat each item. As soon as you feel confident with using these expressions, you can go straight to the exercises.

Tak – Yes

Nie – No

Miło mi cię poznać. – Nice to meet you!

A ty? – And you?/How about you?

Ja też. – Me too.

Ja też nie. – Me neither.

Czy mogę ci jakoś pomóc? – How can I help you?

Nie, dziękuję. – No, thank you.

Myślę, że tak. – I think so.

Myślę, że nie. – I don't think so.

Oczywiście. – Of course/Sure.

Nie ma problemu. – No problem.

Czy mógłbyś/mogłabyś przeliterować? – Could you spell it?

Czy mógłbyś/mogłabyś powtórzyć? – Could you repeat?

Nie rozumiem. – I don't understand.

Powodzenia! – Good luck!

Dobry pomysł! – Good idea!

Myślę, że to dobry pomysł. – I think it's a good idea.

Niech pomyślę… – Let me think…

Poczekaj chwilę. – Wait a moment.

Przepraszam. – Excuse me/I'm sorry

Przepraszam. Muszę już iść. – I'm sorry. I have to go.

Przepraszam za spóźnienie. – Sorry for being late.

Przepraszam, która jest godzina? – Excuse me, what time is it?

Przepraszam, gdzie jest…? – Excuse me, where is…?

Czy mógłbyś/mogłabyś pokazać mi gdzie jest…? – Could you show me where… is?

Czy mógłbyś/mogłabyś pokazać na mapie? – Could you show me on the map?

Here are another two exercises—one easier, and one more difficult. Let's see how well you know the new set:

Exercise: Try to say in Polish the following phrases.

Nice to meet you.

How about you?

Yes.

No.

I think so.

Could you repeat?

Could you spell it?

Good luck!

Wait a moment.

I am sorry.

I don't understand.

Sorry for being late.

Sure.

Me neither.

No problem.

Excuse me.

Excuse me, where is?

How can I help you?

I don't think so.

I don't understand.

Let me think.

Good job! These phrases will definitely make your language journey way easier. Yet knowing them by heart and repeating/translating them will not give you the conversational confidence. Thus, here is a more difficult exercise.

Exercise: Try to say the appropriate Polish phrase based on the context provided. Sometimes there is more than one correct answer. Let your imagination choose what is best.

a) A friend asks you to do him/her a favor. What do you say?

b) The meeting at work has already started. What do you say as soon as you come in?

c) Your friend suggests going to the cinema tonight. What do you say?

d) You don't understand your Polish friend. What do you say?

e) You didn't hear what your friend said, and you want him/her to repeat himself/herself. What do you say?

f) You need to think for a moment. What do you say?

g) You want a stranger to show you a place on the map. What do you say to him/her?

h) You've just met your friend's sister. What do you say to her?

i) You want to apologize for something. What do you say?

j) You want to know what time it is. How do you ask your friend?

k) You want to know what your friend thinks about a certain problem. How do you ask him/her?

l) You see a child crying. What do you say to him/her?

You have just learned some very useful conversational expressions in context. Congratulations! Now it is time to face more linguistic challenges!

Likes/dislikes and Opinion

After introducing yourself and talking about some general facts like your age or place of living, it is time to make your conversation more interesting. The best way to learn something more about a person is to ask him/her some questions concerning interests/likes and dislikes. Thus, we have prepared another important ingredient of a conversation—asking about someone's opinion.

You can ask someone about his/her likes/dislikes in many ways, but let's start from the simplest version. In Polish, it looks like this:

Co lubisz? – What do you like?

Co lubisz najbardziej? – What do you like the most?

A formal version looks like this:

Co Pan/Pani lubi (najbardziej)? – What do you like (the most)?

Co Panie/Panowie/Państwo lubią (najbardziej)? – What do you like (the most)?

If you want to share your opinion, you can say:

Lubię... – I like...

Najbardziej lubię... – I like... the most.

Nie lubię... – I don't like...

Najbardziej nie lubię... – I don't like... the most

Good start! You can use the Polish *lubię/nie lubię* expression when talking not only about things but also activities. Yet you need to keep in mind that formulating these expressions is a bit different compared to English, and we are about to show you in what ways.

At first, let's try to say that you like *ciasto* [a cake].

Lubię ciasto.

Now, try to say that you don't like cake.

Nie lubię ciasta.

What has changed? You have probably noticed that it is no longer *ciasto*, but *ciasta*. The ending has changed since the *nie lubię* phrase requires applying a different case (namely, the genitive).

Unfortunately, Polish cases are so advanced that they would all require writing another book. For now, let's just keep in mind that they exist. Even though you say *nie lubię ciasto* (which is incorrect), your message will be understood anyway—your Polish will just be sounding foreign, that's all.

Now, let's try to say that you like playing football.

Lubię grać w piłkę nożną.

Now you don't like playing football:

Nie lubię grać w piłkę nożną.

Have you noticed the pattern? When talking about activities, the Polish *lubię/nie lubię* phrase always requires an infinitive form of a particular verb. So the literal translation into English would look like this: *I like to play football/I don't like to play football.*

Of course, many other useful words can describe your likes/dislikes, not only *lubię/nie lubię*. Using them will make your Polish usage more advanced and interesting. The rule of using these word is the same as in *lubię/nie lubię*.

Uwielbiam/kocham – I love

Nienawidzę – I hate

Nie cierpię – I can't stand

Wolę/preferuję – I prefer

These are the most popular expressions that will give you a real boost. Try to go through them twice or more in order to remember them.

Uwielbiam/kocham – I love

Nienawidzę – I hate

Nie cierpię – I can't stand

Wolę/preferuję – I prefer

Good job! Now it is time to learn some useful words describing activities. You can apply them to the *like/love/hate* expressions and share your opinion. It is pretty easy! Take your time and learn these expressions carefully. The exercises will be demanding since you are not just a beginner. We have made a list of activities in the infinitive form—since you need to remember that Polish *like/love/hate* phrases require using an infinitive form:

Jeździć na rowerze – to ride a bike

Jeździć konno – to ride a horse

Oglądać telewizję – to watch TV

Chodzić do szkoły – to go to school

Uczyć się – to study

Grać w gry komputerowe – to play computer games

Rysować – to draw

Śpiewać – to sing

Grać na gitarze – to play the guitar

Grać na pianinie – to play the piano

Wychodzić na miasto – to go out

Spędzać czas z przyjaciółmi – to hang out with friends

Chodzić do pracy – to go to work

Jeździć samochodem – to drive a car

Chodzić na siłownię – to go to the gym

Pływać – to swim

Robić grilla – to have a barbeque

Jeść owoce – to eat fruit

Imprezować – to party

Podróżować – to travel

Biegać – to run

Chodzić na spacery – to go for a walk/to walk

Pisać – to write

Czytać książki – to read books

Robić zakupy – to do the shopping

Chodzić do galerii – to go to the shopping center

Excellent! Knowing these activities will make your Polish more advanced! Let's try something more difficult.

Exercise: Try to say in Polish the following expressions.

I like riding a bike.

I hate doing shopping.

I love spending time with my friends.

I don't like running.

I hate reading books.

I love walking.

I like playing the guitar.

I hate singing.

I love riding the horse.

I love going out.

I hate going to school.

I like driving a car.

I love hanging out with my friends.

I love traveling.

I don't like drawing.

I hate studying.

Excellent! Before we move on, let's explore one more thing that might be useful—questions about some specific opinion. In other words, you are about to learn how to ask someone if he/she likes a particular thing. It goes like this:

Lubisz…? – Do you like…?

The rule stays the same. When you ask about activities, they stay in the infinitive form. For example:

Lubisz pływać? – Do you like swimming?

Lubisz jeździć na rowerze? – Do you like riding a bike?

Let's try a short exercise.

Exercise: Try to ask the following questions in Polish.

Do you like singing?

Do you like walking?

Do you like partying?

Do you like drawing?

Do you like going shopping?

Do you like driving a car?

Do you like riding a horse?

Do you like reading books?

Do you like watching TV?

Do you like running?

Do you like playing computer games?

Do you like studying?

Excellent! You are getting more and more confident with your Polish! Now it is time to expand on the likes/dislikes topic and teach you how to express an opinion about things, not activities. Of course, before the exercises, you need to know some basic words that you can use when sharing your opinion. Try to remember as many words as possible.

Below is a list of common food and drink. When it comes to sharing an opinion about things, you need to remember that different cases should be applied. Thus, we have written the forms that need to be used with like/love/hate phrases. Cases are tough but don't get discouraged. Even Polish people struggle with them. Let's begin:

Ziemniaki (ziemniaków) – potatoes

Pomidory (pomidorów) – tomatoes

Ogórki (ogórków)– cucumbers

Papryka czerwona (paprykę czerwoną/papryki czerwonej) – red pepper

Cebula (cebulę/cebuli) – onion

Banan (banana) – banana

Jabłka (jabłek) – apples

Pomarańcza (pomarańczę/pomarańczy) – orange

Grejfrut (grejpfruta) – grapefruit

Cytryna (cytrynę/cytryny) – lemon

Gruszka (gruszkę/gruszki) – pear

Brzoskwinia (brzoskwinię/brzoskwini) – peach

Kiełbasa (kiełbasę/kiełbasy) – sausage

Boczek (boczku) – bacon

Kurczak (kurczaka) – chicken

Czekolada (czekoladę/czekolady) – chocolate

Ciastka (ciastek) – cookies/biscuits

Woda mineralna (wodę mineralną/wody mineralnej) – mineral water

Woda gazowana (wodę gazowaną/wody gazowanej) – sparkling water

Cola (colę/coli) – cola

Czerwone wino (czerwonego wina) – red wine

Białe wino (białego wina) – white wine

Whisky – whiskey

Good job! You don't have to learn by heart different case forms of a particular thing. We will be repeating throughout the whole book that communicative effectiveness is the key. If you want to be 100 percent accurate, your learning process will be much slower. It is good to make mistakes and learn from them.

Now let's try to exercise.

Exercise: Try to say in Polish the following expressions.

I like whiskey.

Do you like chocolate?

Do you like sparkling water?

I don't like bananas.

I don't like mineral water.

I love cola.

I hate white wine.

Do you like red wine?

I love bacon.

I hate sausages.

Do you like apples?

Do you like chicken?

I love cookies.

Do you like orange?

I hate red pepper.

I love cucumbers.

I love grapefruit.

Do you like pear?

Feelings and Emotions

In this section, you will learn how to ask someone about his/her mood and how to express your feelings through the Polish language.

To ask someone about his/her mood or feelings, you need to use the following expression:

Jak się czujesz? – How do you feel?

The polite version looks like this:

Jak się Pan/Pani czuje? – How do you feel? (male/female)

Jak się Panowie/Panie/Państwo czują? – How do you feel? (males/females/males and females)

If you want to tell someone about your mood//feelings, you can use the following expressions:

Jestem ... – I am ...

Czuję się ... – I feel ...

Pretty easy, isn't it? Unfortunately, it is not the whole story though. While the expression itself is quite simple, the word that expresses your feelings introduces some complications. You need to apply a different ending to the adjective, depending on your sex. Males usually apply the ending –y, whereas females apply –a. Without further theoretical explanations, let's go straight into examples since you will grasp the idea based on a real context. Below is a list of basic adjectives describing feelings. On the "Polish side" there are two versions—the first is for males and the second is for females.

Try to remember as many words as possible. You will need them for further practice!

Szczęśliwy/Szczęśliwa – happy

Smutny/smutna – sad

Zmęczony/zmęczona – tired

Pewny/pewna siebie – confident

Poekscytowany/podekscytowana – excited

Zainteresowany/zainteresowana – interested

Zaskoczony/zaskoczona – surprised

Znudzony/znudzona – bored

Zdenerwowany/zdenerwowana – nervous

Głodny/głodna – hungry

Spragniony/spragniona – thirsty

Śpiący/śpiąca – sleepy

Chory/chora – sick

Obolały/obolała – sore

Oszołomiony/oszołomiona – dizzy

Wkurzony/wkurzona – angry

Usatysfakcjonowany/usatysfakcjonowana – satisfied

Dumny/dumna – proud

Sfrustrowany/sfustrowana – frustrated

Przestraszony/przestraszona – scared

Rozczarowany/rozczarowana – disappointed

Good job! It is time to practice these words in a real context. Remember about choosing a form that corresponds with your sex.

Exercise: Try to say the following phrases in Polish.

I feel tired.

I am hungry.

How do you feel?

I feel angry!

How do you feel? (formal, male)

I feel dizzy.

I am surprised.

How do you feel? (formal, female)

I feel sick.

I am excited.

How do you feel? (formal, males)

I feel thirsty.

I am proud.

How do you feel? (formal, females)

I feel sore.

I am confident.

How do you feel? (formal, males and females)

I feel bored.

I am disappointed.

I feel sleepy.

I am nervous.

I am sad.

I feel happy.

I am scared.

Very good! If you have problems with a particular structure, don't hesitate to go back to the previous chapters. Learning a foreign language is a demanding process and takes time.

Before we go on to the next chapter, here are some exercises as a revision of the knowledge you have already acquired. Prepare yourself for multiskill practice! If you feel confident enough and don't need more time, try these exercises now.

Revision

This section is designed to test your knowledge and everything you have already learned about the Polish language. The exercises contain items and expressions picked randomly from different sections.

Exercise 1 – Try to say the following expressions in Polish:

I love walking.

I like playing the guitar.

I hate singing.

I love riding the horse.

I love going out.

I hate going to school.

I like driving a car.

I feel sore.

I am confident.

How do you feel? (formal, males and females)

I feel bored.

I am disappointed.

I feel sleepy.

I am nervous.

I am sad.

Do you like singing?

Do you like walking?

Do you like partying?

Do you like drawing?

Wait a moment.

I am sorry.

I don't understand.

Sorry for being late.

Sure.

Me neither.

No problem.

Excuse me.

I am 97 years old.

I am 6 years old.

I am 45 years old.

I am 23 years old.

I live in a house.

I live in a block of flats.

I live in the city center.

I live in the mountains.

I live near a big city.

Exercise 2 – There will be a couple of guided dialogs with English expressions to translate. Try to say everything in Polish.

Dialog 1:

- Hello. I am Sarah.

- Hello. I am Ania. How old are you?

- I am 16. And you?

- I am 23. Where are you from?

- I am from the USA, and you?

- I am from Poland.

- Nice to meet you.

Dialog 2:

- What do you like the most?

- I like riding a bike and play computer games. And you?

- I like riding a bike and singing. I don't like playing computer games.

- Okay. I don't like doing shopping.

Dialog 3:

- Where are you from?

- I am from Poland, and you?

- I am from England. Where do you live?

- I live in Warsaw. And you?

- I live in London.

Dialog 4:

- How do you feel?

- I feel tired. And you?

- I am hungry. What do you like?

- I like ice cream and bananas, and you?

- I like chicken and cola.

Exercise 3 – There will be a couple of situations that will require different expressions, but you won't be provided with the English versions. The only thing you will know is the context. Try to come up with Polish expressions based on the context provided:

- You want to apologize for something. What do you say?

- You want to know what time it is. How do you ask your friend?

- You want to know what your friend thinks about a certain problem. How do you ask him/her?

- You see a child crying. What do you say to him/her?

- You've just met your friend's brother. Introduce yourself, say a couple of phrases about yourself (your place of living/your age) and ask him how old he is.

- You are talking about favorite foods with your friend. Tell him/her what you like the most and ask him/her what he/she likes the most.

- You are talking about favorite ways of spending free time with your friend. Tell him/her what you like the most and ask what he/she likes the most.

- You've just met your new boss. Introduce yourself, tell him/her about your place of living/your age, and ask him/her how he/she feels.

- Your friend wants to know how you feel today. Tell him/her and ask how he/she feels today.

- Your teacher is asking you how you feel. Tell him/her and ask how he/she feels today.

- You've just met your new teacher. Introduce yourself, tell a couple of things about your age/place of living, etc.

- Ask your friend's parents about their favorite ways of spending free time.

- Ask your coworker about his/her favorite food.

- You got lost in the city center. Introduce yourself to a stranger and tell him/her where you are from. Then, ask him/her to show you the way on the map.

Good job! You are confident enough to have a basic conversation in Polish. With such knowledge, you will be able to use Polish in different situations, formal and informal. This chapter has equipped you with the basic skills that will be helpful no matter what situation you will be faced with.

Chapter 6 – At Work

If you have got this far, you've probably learned the basics of the Polish language. In this chapter, you are going to learn vocabulary connected to jobs and the working environment as well as some useful phrases.

Profession

No matter where you live, questions concerning your way of living appear very often. It is good to know how they sound in Polish, so here they are:

Gdzie pracujesz? – Where do you work?

Kim jesteś z zawodu? – What is your profession?

Co robisz w życiu? – What do you do? (general question)

If you want to tell someone about your profession, you need to use the following phrases:

Jestem... – I am a/an...*

Pracuję jako... – I work as a...

*The phrase *jestem...* requires using a different case, whereas the phrase *pracuję jako...* does not change the case of the noun. To

show how these phrases work, let's take the word *lekarz* [doctor].
The first phrase would look like this:

Jestem lekarz**em**.

The second phrase would look like this:

Pracuję jako lekarz.

As always, using the wrong case will not entirely affect the understanding of your message. You don't have to learn all the declensions. The best way to master the inflectional system is to use the language and learn from your mistakes.

Now it is time to learn some new vocabulary. Below is a list of popular professions. Go through the list multiple times and try to remember as many words as possible. We have included the second form to allow you the opportunity to practice both ways of telling someone about your profession.

Professions:

Lekarz (lekarzem) – a doctor

Nauczyciel (nauczycielem) – a teacher

Biznesmen (biznesmenem) – a businessman

Bizneswoman (bizneswoman) – a businesswoman

Prawnik (prawnikiem)– a lawyer

Pielęgniarka (pielęgniarką) – a nurse

Sprzedawca (sprzedawcą) – a shop assistant

Księgowy/księgowa (księgowym/księgową) – an accountant

Strażak (strażakiem) – a firefighter

Żołnierz (żołnierzem) – a soldier

Policjant (policjantem) – a policeman

Policjantka (policjantką) – a policewoman

Szef kuchni (szefem kuchni) – a chef

Kucharz (kucharzem) – a cook

Kelner (kelnerem) – a waiter

Kelnerka (kelnerką) – a waitress

Pilot (pilotem) – a pilot

Naukowiec (naukowcem) – a scientist

Listonosz (listonoszem)– a postman

Tłumacz (tłumaczem) – a translator

Mechanik (mechanikiem) – a mechanic

Hydraulik (hydraulikiem)– a plumber

Malarz (malarzem) – a painter

Aktor (aktorem) – an actor

Aktorka (aktorką) – an actress

Kierowca (kierowcą) – a driver

Sprzątacz/sprzątaczka (sprzątaczem/sprzątaczką) – a cleaner

Dentysta (dentystą) – a dentist

Rolnik (rolnikiem) – a farmer

Inżynier (inżynierem) – an engineer

Kierownik/menedżer (kierownikiem/menadżerem) – a manager

Fotograf (fotografem) – a photographer

Muzyk (muzykiem) – a musician

Sekretarz/sekretarka (sekretarzem/sekretarką) – a secretary

Kierowca taksówki (kierowcą taksówki) – a taxi driver

Pisarz (pisarzem) – a writer

Opiekun/opiekunka (opiekunem/opiekunką) – a babysitter

Piekarz (piekarzem) – a baker

Fryzjer (fryzjerem) – a hairdresser

Filmowiec (filmowcem) – a filmmaker

Dziennikarz (dziennikarzem) – a journalist

Ksiądz (księdzem) – a priest

Weterynarz (weterynarzem) – a vet

Psycholog (psychologiem) – a psychologist

Badacz (badaczem) – a researcher

Exercise: Try to say the following phrases in Polish.

I am a researcher.

I work as a dentist.

I work as a firefighter.

I am an actor.

I work as a filmmaker.

I am a waiter.

I am a waitress.

I work as an accountant.

I am a businessman.

I am a businesswoman.

I work as a cleaner.

I am a cook.

I work as a hairdresser.

I work as a plumber.

I am a taxi driver.

I am a journalist.

I work as a mechanic.

I am a farmer.

Good job! You have learned how to tell someone about your profession. Now it is time to move on to some advanced vocabulary connected to the work environment and some specific phrases that will make you more confident with your Polish.

Working Environment

It is time to learn some advanced phrases! At first, we will give you some vocabulary. After learning some essential words, you will have the opportunity to learn some phrases that might be very useful, especially if you are planning to work in Poland. Let's start!

Miejsce pracy – workplace

Biuro – office

Praca – job

Fabryka – factory

Firma – company

Siedziba firmy – headquarters

Korporacja – corporation

Pracownik – employee

Pracodawca – employer

Szef/szefowa – boss

Koledzy z pracy – colleagues/coworkers

Praca zdalna – remote working

Pracownik fizyczny – blue-collar worker

Pracować – work

Wypłata – salary

Zarobki – earnings/wages

Brutto – gross

Netto – post-tax

Podatek – tax

Awans – promotion

Dostać awans – to get a promotion

Dostać pracę – to get a job

Być zwolnionym – to be dismissed

Być zwolnionym natychmiastowo – to be fired

Zredukować personel – to make people redundant

Podwyżka – pay rise

Dostać podwyżkę – to get a pay rise

Praca na cały etat – full-time job

Praca na pół etatu – part-time job

Praca dodatkowa – side job

Praca zmianowa – shift job

Nocna zmiana/nocka – night shift

Rozmowa o pracę – job interview

Umowa o pracę – job agreement

Życiorys (CV) – curriculum vitae (CV)

Podanie o pracę – job application form

Stanowisko – position

Kwalifikacje – qualifications

Wymagania – requirements

Umiejętności – skills

Wykształcenie – education

Doświadczenie zawodowe – job experience

Dział kadr – personnel department/HR

Dział obsługi klienta – customer service department

Dział wsparcia technicznego – help desk

Wyjazd służbowy – business trip

Notatka służbowa – memo

Spotkanie – meeting

Urlop – leave

Urlop macierzyński – maternity leave

Urlop zdrowotny – sick leave

Urlop bezpłatny – unpaid leave

Płatny urlop wypoczynkowy – paid vacation leave

It is time to practice and memorize the words! Let's check what you remember.

Exercise: Try to find the English equivalents for these Polish words.

Korporacja

Pracownik

Pracodawca

Szef/szefowa

Kwalifikacje

Wymagania

Umiejętności

Notatka służbowa

Spotkanie

Urlop

Pracować

Wypłata

Zarobki

Brutto

Netto

Podatek

Doświadczenie zawodowe

Dział kadr

Dział obsługi klienta

Dział wsparcia technicznego

Wyjazd służbowy

Dostać awans

Dostać pracę

Być zwolnionym

Być zwolnionym natychmiastowo

Praca na cały etat

Praca na pół etatu

Excellent! You have learned plenty of essential words that will help you survive in the Polish working environment! Now it is time to go further and learn some very useful phrases. Take your time and repeat them multiple times. Try to remember as many phrases as possible.

Proszę przesłać CV oraz podanie o pracę. – Please, send your CV and a job application form.

Pracuję na pół etatu. – I have a part-time job.

Pracuję w dużej firmie. – I work in a big company.

Jestem nauczycielem/nauczycielką. Pracuję w szkole średniej. – I am a teacher. I work at a high school.

Gdzie znajduje się firma w której pracujesz? – Where is the company you work at located?

Firma znajduje się w Warszawie. – The company headquarters is located in Warsaw.

Pracuję w systemie zmianowym. – I have a shift job.

O której godzinie kończysz pracę? – What time do you finish your work?

Dziś kończę o 17:00. – Today I'm finishing at 5:00 pm.

Dziś idę na nockę. – Today I'm working a night shift.

Jakie wykształcenie Pan/Pani posiada? – What educational background do you have?

Ukończyłem/ukończyłam uniwersytet. – I graduated/graduated university.

Jakie umiejętności Pan/Pani posiada? – What skills do you have?

Czy posiada Pan/Pani prawo jazdy? – Do you have a driving license?

Tak, posiadam prawo jazdy. – Yes, I have a driving license.

Jakie jest Pana/Pani doświadczenie zawodowe? – What is your job experience?

Pracowałem dla firmy... od 2011 roku. – I worked for the company... since 2011.

Prosimy skontaktować się z naszym działem wsparcia technicznego. – Please, contact our help desk.

Proszę przesłać podanie o pracę do działu kadr. – Please, send your application form to the personnel department.

Dostałem/dostałam awans! – I got a promotion!

Czy mogę wziąć dzień wolnego? – Can I take a day off?

Jestem chory/chora. Jutro nie mogę przyjść do pracy. – I am sick. I can't go to work tomorrow.

Good job! Now it is time to practice. However, we haven't made it easy—you need to come up with a Polish phrase on your own, not to translate directly from English!

Exercise: Try to come up with a suitable Polish phrase. There are no straight answers—everything depends on your imagination!

    a) Ask your colleague what time he/she finishes his/her job

    b) Tell your friends that you got a promotion

    c) Tell your interviewer that you've graduated from university

    d) Ask your boss to give you a day off

    e) Tell your boss that you are sick and you can't go to work tomorrow

    f) Tell your friend what time you finish work

    g) Tell your interviewer that you have a driving license

    h) Tell your business partner about the location of your company's headquarters

    i) Tell your interviewer about your previous job experience.

Good job! You are confident enough to join the Polish working environment. There is much more to learn, yet knowing these phrases and words will give you a good start.

Chapter 7 – At School/At The University

Due to globalization and open borders, especially in the European Union, many students have the opportunity to study abroad. Many interesting exchange programs enable you to spend a year in a different country while learning the same subjects. Even some younger learners can go abroad on their own by taking part in a language camp or a school trip.

If you are considering choosing Poland as your target country, it is a good choice! Even though most of your friends will speak English, you need to familiarize yourself with some essential vocabulary and phrases that will help you survive the first days/weeks in a Polish school. Thus, we have chosen the most important Polish words or phrases that you might be faced with during your school trip/exchange year. Here we go!

School subjects

You will probably feel lost during your first days in a completely different environment, especially while looking for classrooms, classes, and teachers. It is good to know your lesson plan in advance;

thus, the following list includes a list of school subjects that you definitely need to know:

Edukacja – education

Język polski – Polish

Matematyka – mathematics/maths

Język obcy – foreign language

Język angielski – English

Język niemiecki – German

Język hiszpański – Spanish

Geografia – geography

Historia – history

Biologia – biology

Chemia – chemistry

Fizyka – physics

Religia – religion

Wychowanie fizyczne (WF) – physical education (PE)

Muzyka – music class

Plastyka – art class

Informatyka – IT class

Godzina wychowawcza – form period/homeroom period

Zajęcia dodatkowe – extracurricular activities

Kółko zainteresowań – special interest group

Zajęcia wyrównawcze – remedial class

Gimnastyka korekcyjna – remedial exercises

Zajęcia praktyczne – practical class

Zajęcia do wyboru – elective courses

Zajęcia wychowawcze – advisory class

Zajęcia wieczorowe – night class

Exercise: Try to come up with an English equivalent of the following Polish school subject.

Geografia

Historia

Biologia

Chemia

Fizyka

Religia

Język polski

Matematyka

Język obcy

Język angielski

Religia

Wychowanie fizyczne (WF)

Muzyka

Plastyka

Informatyka

Zajęcia praktyczne

Zajęcia do wyboru

Zajęcia wychowawcze

Zajęcia wieczorowe

Good job! Knowing your lesson plan will give you confidence during your first days at school. Yet to make your experience even less stressful, you need to know some basic words connected to the school environment. As always, try to remember as many words as possible and go through the list multiple times.

School Environment

Nauczyciel – teacher

Uczeń – student

Dyrektor szkoły – school head teacher/school principal

Sala lekcyjna – classroom

Lekcja – lesson

Zajęcia – class

Stołówka – cafeteria/canteen

Sklepik szkolny – tuck shop

Szatnia – changing room

Sala gimnastyczna – school gym

Boisko szkolne – school playground

Sekretariat szkolny – school's secretary office

Biblioteka szkolna – school library

Czytelnia – a reading room

Sala komputerowa – IT suite

Gabinet dyrektora – head teacher's office

Woźny – caretaker

Dzwonek szkolny – school bell

Przerwa – break

Przerwa śniadaniowa – lunch break

Świetlica szkolna – afterschool club

Autobus szkolny – school bus

Wycieczka szkolna – school trip

Sprawdzian/test – test

Ocena – grade (oceny – grades)

Kartkówka – short quiz

Egzamin państwowy – state exam

Uczyć się – to learn/to study

Uczyć się na pamięć – to learn by heart

Wkuwać – swot/cram

Zaliczyć/zdać test – to pass a test

Oblać test/nie zaliczyć testu – to fail a test

Pisać egzamin – to take a test

Poprawiać test – to retake a test

Egzamin poprawkowy/poprawka – retake

Dziennik lekcyjny – register

Prezentacja – presentation

Egzamin ustny – oral exam

Egzamin pisemny – written exam

Zadanie domowe – homework

Projekt – project

Praca w grupach – group work

Praca w parach – pair work

Rozmowa – conversation

Dyskusja – discussion

There have been many new words to memorize; thus, it is time to practice and ensure that you have made the most of your learning.

Exercise: Try to come up with a Polish equivalent of the following English words.

IT suite

head teacher's office

caretaker

school bell

break

to fail a test

to take a test

to retake a test

retake

register

changing room

school gym

school playground

school's secretary office

school library

oral exam

written exam

homework

project

group work

teacher

student

school head teacher/school principal

classroom

Excellent! You have made huge progress and communication in Polish. To give you a boost, below are some essential phrases that might be very useful during your Polish schooldays. Take your time and repeat each phrase a few times:

Dzień dobry, uczniowie! – Good morning, students!

Dzień dobry, Panie/Pani... – Good morning, Mr./Mrs./Ms.

Siadajcie, proszę. – Sit down, please.

Otwórzcie podręczniki na stronie 46. – Please, open your books on page 46.

W pyszłym tygodniu odbędzie się kartkówka ze słówek. – Next week there will be a short vocabulary quiz.

Przepraszam, czy mogę wyjść do toalety? – Excuse me, can I go to the toilet?

Zadania 3, 4, 5 to zadanie domowe na przyszły tydzień. – Exercises 3, 4, 5 are homework for the next week.

Robert, czy mógłbyś wytrzeć tablicę? – Robert, could you clean the blackboard, please?

Dziś będziemy mówić o dzikich zwierzętach. – Today we will be talking about wild animals.

Czy mógłbyś to przeliterować? – Could you spell it out?

Przepraszam, gdzie jest stołówka? – Excuse me, where is the school canteen?

Przepraszam, jak dojdę do sali gimnastycznej? – Excuse me, how can I get to the gym?

O której kończy się lekcja? – What time does the lesson end?

Lekcja kończy się o godzinie 9:45. – The lesson ends at 9:45 am.

Jakie przedmioty mamy dzisiaj? – Which classes do we have today?

Dzisiaj mamy matematykę, fizykę, informatykę, WF i geografię. – Today we have maths, physics, IT, PE, and geography.

O której godzinie odjeżdża autobus szkolny? – What time does the school bus leave?

Autobus szkolny odjeżdża o 15:00, zaraz po ostatniej lekcji. – The school bus leaves at 3:00 pm, right after the last lesson.

Dzisiejsze zajęcia są odwołane. – Today's classes have been canceled.

Now it is time to practice a bit. We won't ask you for a translation; you will need to come up with a suitable phrase on your own.

Exercise: Try to come up with a suitable Polish phrase. There are no straight answers—everything depends on your imagination!

a) You don't know what time the school bus leaves. Ask your friend.

b) You don't know what time the lesson ends. Ask your friend.

c) You don't know what classes you have today. Ask your friend.

d) You had a problem with understanding a word. Ask your friend to spell it out.

e) You don't know where the school canteen is. Ask your friend.

f) Your PE lesson is starting in five minutes, but you don't know where the gym is. Ask your friend to give you directions.

g) Your friend wants to know what time the school bus leaves. Tell him/her.

h) Your teacher wants to know your name. Introduce yourself.

i) Your friend wants to know what classes your class has today. Tell him/her.

j) Your friend wants to know what time the lesson ends. Tell him/her.

At the University/College

Whether you have decided to study in Poland or take part in a student exchange program, it doesn't matter. Poland is a beautiful country, and you will enjoy your stay. In order not to get lost, it is advisable to know at least some basic words and phrases connected to the academic environment:

Uniwersytet – University/college

Stopień naukowy – degree

Student – student

Wykładowca – lecturer

Wykład – lecture

Sala wykładowa – lecture room

Aula – lecture hall

Licencjat – bachelor's degree

Magister – master's degree

Dyplom/świadectwo – diploma

Zajęcia praktyczne – practicals

Praktykant – trainee

Notatki – notes

Robić notatki – to take notes

Wygłaszać mowę – to give a speech

Przygotowywać prezentację – to prepare a presentation

Badanie – research/study

Przeprowadzać badanie – to conduct research

Wyniki badania – results of the study

Rektor uniwersytetu – college president/university president

Egzamin – exam

Sesja egzaminacyjna – exam session

Zaliczenie warunkowe – conditional promotion

Rok studiów – college level

Praca dyplomowa – thesis

Praca licencjacka – bachelor's thesis/BA thesis

Praca magisterska – master's thesis/MA thesis

Studia zaoczne – part-time studies

Studia dzienne – full-time studies

Kampus uniwersytecki – the university campus

Dziekanat – deanery/dean's office

Doktorat – doctorate

Praca doktorancka – Ph.D. thesis

Absolwent – graduate

Absolutorium – graduation ceremony

Wydział – institute

Władze szkoły – school authorities

Rekrutacja – recruitment

Egzaminy wstępne – entrance exams

Wymiana studencka – student exchange program

Indeks – student book

Legtymacja studencka – student ID card

Kredyt studencki – student loan

Akademik – residence hall/dormitory

Europejski System Transferu Punktów (ECTS) – European Credit Transfer System (ECTS)

Good! However, if you don't feel confident enough, go back over these and try to repeat them out loud as many times as possible. Eventually, all these new words won't be new at all.

Time to practice!

Exercise: Try to find the English equivalents of the following Polish words.

Praca licencjacka

Praca magisterska

Studia zaoczne

Studia dzienne

Wymiana studencka

Indeks

Legitymacja studencka

Kredyt studencki

Akademik

Rektor uniwersytetu

Egzamin

Sesja egzaminacyjna

Student

Wykładowca

Wykład

Sala wykładowa

Aula

Praktykant

Notatki

Robić notatki

Excellent! You have learned many new words connected with the academic environment. To feel even more confident with your Polish, you need to learn some phrases. Below are some expressions that might help you during your college days/exchange. There are many of them, but don't get discouraged. Try to remember as many as possible and repeat them out loud:

Przepraszam, gdzie znajduje się dziekanat? – Excuse me, where is the dean's office?

Dziekanat znajduje się na trzecim piętrze. – The dean's office is on the third floor.

Przepraszam, gdzie znajduje się aula C1? – Excuse me, where is the lecture hall C1?

Aula C1 jest na czwartym piętrze. – C1 is on the fourth floor.

Dzisiejsze wykłady są odwołane. – All of today's lectures have been canceled.

Wyniki egzaminów zimowych są dostępne na stronie internetowej wydziału. – Winter exams results are available on the website of our institute.

Ten wykład jest nieobowiązkowy. – This lecture is non-mandatory.

Przepraszam, o której rozpoczyna się ostatni wykład? – Excuse me, what time does the last lecture start?

Ostati wykład zaczyna się o 17:00. – The last lecture starts at 5:00 pm.

Dzień dobry, chciałbym/chciałabym wypożyczyć książkę. – Hello, I would like to borrow a book.

Jaka książka Pana/Panią interesuje? – What book are you looking for?

Szukam… – I am looking for…

Proszę chwilkę poczekać. – Wait a moment, please.

Czy to jest książka, której Pan/Pani szuka? – Is that the book you are looking for?

Tak, to dokładnie ta. – Yes, exactly.

Czy mogę zobaczyć Pana/Pani legitymację studencką? – May I see your student ID card?

Oczywiście, proszę. – Of course, here you are.

Dzień dobry, chciałbym/chciałabym wziąć udział w wymianie studenckiej. – Hello, I would like to take part in a student exchange program.

Jaki kraj chciałby Pan/chciałaby Pan odwiedzić? – What country would you like to visit?

Jestem zainteresowany/zainteresowana studiowaniem w Polsce. – I am interested in studying in Poland.

Świetny wybór! Może Pan/Pani skorzystać z naszego nowego programu trwającego pół roku. – Great choice! You can take part in our new program that is a half year long.

Jakie uczelnie w Polsce mogę wybrać? – Which Polish universities can I choose?

Czy w Polsce będę musiał/musiała zdawać egzaminy? – Do I have to take all the exams in Poland?

Tak, wszystkie egzaminy będzie musiał Pan/musiała Pani napisać w Polsce. – Yes, you will have to take all the exams in Poland.

Czy mogą wziąć udział w programie na ostatnim roku studiów? – Can I take part in the exchange program in the last year of my studies?

Niestety, nie może Pan/Pani wziąć udziału w wymianie na ostatnim roku. – I'm sorry, you can't take part in the exchange in the last year.

Dlaczego? – Why?

Ponieważ musi Pan/Pani przeprowadzić badanie i napisać pracę tutaj. – Because you have to conduct the study and write your thesis here.

Exercise: Try to come up with a suitable Polish phrase. There are no straight answers—everything depends on your imagination!

> a) You are looking for the lecture room D2. Ask your friend where it is.
>
> b) Tell the librarian that you want to borrow a book.
>
> c) Tell the college employee that you want to take part in a student exchange program.
>
> d) You want to know if you have to take all the exams. Ask your lecturer.
>
> e) You don't know what time the lecture starts. Ask your friend.
>
> f) Your friend wants to know if the next lecture is mandatory. Tell him/her that it isn't.
>
> g) Your friend wants to know what time the last lecture starts. Tell him/her.
>
> h) Tell your friends that all lectures have been canceled today.
>
> i) You are looking for the dean's office. Ask your friend to show you where it is.
>
> j) Tell the college employee that you want to study in Poland.

Excellent! The above words and phrases will help you survive in the Polish academic environment, at least during the first weeks. If you don't feel confident enough, go through the exercises and lists again and again.

Chapter 8 – Food and Drink

Food and drink are one of the most important things on your trip to a foreign country. Whether you are going to eat out or cook at a hostel/apartment, you will have to know some basic vocabulary. Here are the most essential words:

Dairy Products – produkty mleczne:

Mleko – milk

Śmietana – cream

Ser żółty – cheese

Twarożek – cottage cheese

Jogurt – yogurt

Masło – butter

Margaryna – margarine

Maślanka – buttermilk

Bakery – pieczywo:

Chleb – bread

Chleb pszenny – wheat bread

Świeży chleb – fresh bread

Chleb żytni – rye bread

Chleb tostowy – toast bread

Bułka – bread roll

Bagietka – baguette

Pączki – donuts

Ciastka – biscuits/cookies

Vegetables – warzywa:

Ziemniak – potato

Pomidor – tomato

Ogórek – cucumber

Papryka czerwona – red pepper

Cebula – onion

Kapusta – cabbage

Sałata – lettuce

Marchewka – carrot

Brokuł – broccoli

Kalafior – cauliflower

Fasola – beans

Czosnek – garlic

Dynia – pumpkin

Szpinak – spinach

Pietruszka – parsley

Soja – soy

Seler – celery

Jarmuż – kale

Burak – beet/beetroot

Batat – sweet potato

Fruits – owoce:

Banan – banana

Jabłko – apple

Pomarańcza – orange

Grejfrut – grapefruit

Cytryna – lemon

Gruszka – pear

Brzoskwinia – peach

Kokos – coconut

Ananas – pineapple

Śliwka – plum

Arbuz – watermelon

Truskawka – strawberry

Malina – raspberry

Jagoda – blueberry

Wiśnia – cherry

Awokado – avocado

Orzech włoski – a walnut

Meat – mięso:

Kiełbasa – sausage

Bekon – bacon

Kurczak – chicken

Drób – poultry

Wołowina – beef

Wieprzowina – pork

Baranina – lamb

Szynka – ham

Mięso mielone – minced meat

Kabanos – a kabanos sausage (a snack stick sausage)

Salami – salami

Sweets/Candy – słodycze:

Czekolada – chocolate

Ciastka – cookies/biscuits

Cukierki czekoladowe – bonbons

Delicje – jaffa cakes

Batonik – chocolate bar

Żelki – jelly beans/gummy bears

Deser – dessert

Galaretka – jelly

Wafelek – wafer

Lody – ice cream

Lizak – lollipop

Krówka – fudge

Landrynki – hard candy

Beverages – napoje:

Woda w butelce – bottled water

Woda mineralna – mineral water

Woda gazowana – sparkling water

Cola – cola

Napoje gazowane – fizzy drinks

Sok pomarańczowy – orange juice

Sok jabłkowy – apple juice

Koktajl owocowy – fruit cocktail/smoothie

Kawa – coffee

Kawa rozpuszczalna – instant coffe

Kawa czarna – black coffee

Kawa z mlekiem – white coffee

Herbata – tea

Gorąca czekolada – hot chocolate

Piwo – beer

Wódka – vodka

Czerwone wino – red wine

Białe wino – white wine

Whisky – whiskey

Other Groceries:

Jajka – eggs

Mąka – flour

Sól – salt

Pieprz – pepper

Cukier – sugar

Cukier brązowy – cane sugar

Ryż – rice

Olej – oil

Oliwa z oliwek – olive oil

Przyprawy – spices

Miód – honey

Płatki kukurydziane – corn flakes

Płatki śniadaniowe – cereal

Go through the list many times and repeat each word out loud. It is good to know at least some basic names since many grocery shops in Poland are not like supermarkets. When you want to buy something in a small shop, you need to go straight to the shop assistant and tell him or her what you want. Otherwise, you won't be able to buy anything.

When it comes to Polish supermarkets, they are quite common too; you can find at least one, even in a small town. When it comes to the bigger cities, there are many supermarkets everywhere; however, they are not as big as the American ones. One of the most popular Polish supermarkets is Biedronka [the Ladybird]. You will also find some foreign supermarkets, such as Tesco, Lidl, Kaufland, Intermarche, and Carrefour, and some smaller franchises, such as Żabka [the Frog], Stokrotka [the Daisy], Małpka [the Monkey], and Polo Market.

For now, let's pretend that you are not in a supermarket but a small grocery shop. You want to cook something in the shared kitchen in your hostel and are looking for the ingredients. Your task is simple—you need to tell the shop assistant what you want.

If you want to buy something, you need to say:

Poproszę... – please...

Exercise: Try to buy products from your shopping list. The shop assistant doesn't know a word of English!

   a) Eggs, flour, sugar, mineral water, honey, and cereal

   b) Tea, chocolate, beer, bread, and yogurt

c) Parsley, apple, sausage, ham, and milk

d) Rice, salt, pepper, tomatoes, and potatoes

e) Ice cream, avocado, fresh bread, and butter

Good job! It is important to know that you need to use polite language while speaking with a shop assistant. So don't say *cześć!*— use *dzień dobry!/do widzenia* instead.

Here are more phrases that might be useful while doing shopping:

Przepraszam, ile to kosztuje? – Excuse me, how much does it cost?

Czy mogę zapłacić gotówką? – Can I pay with cash?

Czy chciałby Pan/chciałaby Pani zapłacić kartą czy gotówką? – Would you like to pay with cash or with a credit card?

Czy mogę prosić o paragon? – Can I have a receipt, please?

Proszę wprowadzić PIN. – Enter your PIN code, please.

Dziś polecamy… – I recommend buying… today.

Ok, wezmę to. – Okay, I'll take it.

Nie, dziękuję. – No, thanks.

Czy mogę zwrócić ten produkt? – Can I return this product?

Przepraszam, gdzie znajdę owoce? – Excuse me, where can I find fruit?

Tak, w sekcji artykułów spożywczych – Yes, they are in the produce section.

Czy chciałby Pan/chciałaby Pani torbę? – Would you like a plastic bag?

Ten produkt jest obecnie wyprzedany. – This item is currently out of stock.

Czy ten produkt jest w promocji? – Is this product on sale?

Chciałbym/Chciałabym zapłacić gotówką. – I would like to pay with cash.

Chciałbym/Chciałabym zapłacić kartą. – I would like to pay with a credit card.

Proszę, oto reszta. – Here's your change.

Czy jest Pan/Pani członkiem naszego klubu? – Are you a member of our loyalty program?

Czy ma Pan/Pani jakieś drobne? – Have you got any change?*

*Keep in mind: It's quite common that cashiers in Poland ask about the change. If you buy only one thing and give them a bank note, you might be asked to provide some change.

It is time to practice! All you need to do is to react in Polish:

  a) Tell the shop assistant that you want your receipt.

  b) You want to know if a particular product is on sale. Ask the shop assistant.

  c) You're looking for fresh bread. Ask the shop assistant to tell you where it is.

  d) Tell the shop assistant that you want to pay with cash.

  e) Tell the shop assistant that you want to pay with a credit card.

  f) Ask the shop assistant whether you can return a product.

  g) Buy eggs (by telling the shop assistant that you want to)

  h) Buy fresh bread (by telling the shop assistant that you want to)

  i) Buy coffee (by telling the shop assistant that you want to)

  j) Buy mineral water (by telling the shop assistant that you want to)

Good job! You are no longer afraid of doing shopping, even in small grocery shops. If you want to use your Polish and practice, we recommend only choosing small shops.

At the Restaurant

When you visit a different country, you probably want to try its cuisine. The best way to do this is to visit restaurants and cafés. Even though most of the staff will probably speak fluent English, it is nice to, at least, say "Thank you!" in the foreign language when visiting a restaurant. And if you go to less known places, don't be surprised when your waiter won't understand English! After all, knowing some basic vocabulary used at a restaurant will make you more confident during your trip to Poland. The following words and phrases will make your trip to a Polish restaurant way easier:

Menu – menu

Śniadanie – breakfast

Lunch – lunch

Obiad – dinner

Kolacja – supper

Przystawki – starters/appetizers

Danie główne – main course/main dish

Zimne napoje – cold drinks

Gorące napoje – hot drinks

Kelner – waiter

Kelnerka – waitress

Szef kuchni – chef

Rachunek – bill

Rezerwacja – reservation

Danie dnia – today's special/dish of the day

Zarezerwować stolik – to book a table

Zapłacić gotówką – to pay with cash

Zapłacić kartą – to pay with a credit card

Złożyć zamówienie – to place the order

Napiwek – a tip (leaving huge tips or leaving tips at all is not a very common thing in Poland. If you don't leave a tip, it is absolutely fine).

Exercise: Say in Polish the following words.

lunch

dinner

supper

starters/appetizers

main course/main dish

cold drinks

hot drinks

waiter

waitress

chef

bill

reservation

today's special/dish of the day

Good! Now it is time to learn some phrases that will enable you to order a meal and communicate with the waiter/waitress in Polish:

Dzień dobry, chciałbym/chciałabym zarezerwować stolik dla ... osób. – Good morning, I would like to book a table for... people.

Dobry wieczór, mam rezerwację dla dwóch osób. – Good evening, I have a reservation for two people.

Dzień dobry, czy mogę przyjąć zamówienie? – Good morning, can I take your order?

Chciałbym/Chaciałabym… – I would like…

Czy mógłby/mogłaby mi Pan/Pani polecić coś do jedzenia? – Could you recommend something to eat?

Czy mógłby/mogłaby mi Pan/Pani polecić coś do jedzenia? – Could you recommend something to drink?

Czy chciałby/ chciałaby Pan/Pani coś do picia? – Would you like something to drink?

Przepraszam, czy mogę dostać menu? – Excuse me, can I have a menu, please?

Jakie jest dzisiejsze danie dnia? – What dish is today's special?

Chciałbym/chciałabym zapłacić kartą. – I would like to pay with a credit card.

Chciałbym/chciałabym zapłacić gotówką. – I would like to pay with cash.

Chciałbym/Chciałabym zapłacić. – I would like to pay.*

*The service in Polish restaurants looks slightly different; don't expect your waiter to come to you every five minutes and check if everything is okay with the meal. If you want to pay, you just need to call the waiter and say that you want your bill.

Now it is time to practice. As always, try to choose the best Polish phrase:

   a) Tell your waiter/waitress that you want a menu.

   b) You want to know what is today's special. Ask your waiter.

   c) Tell your waiter/waitress that you want to pay.

d) Tell your waiter/waitress that you want to pay with cash.

e) Tell your waiter/waitress that you want to pay with a credit card.

f) Book a table for five people.

g) Ask your waiter to recommend something to eat.

h) Ask your waiter to recommend something to drink.

Excellent! If you want to order a particular meal, you just say *poproszę* + the name of the meal (just as in the shopping section). For example:

Poproszę kawę. – One coffee, please.

Remember that *poproszę* changes the case of the noun (here: the name of a meal/product). Yet if you forget about applying the case (accusative), you will be understood anyway. Just don't feel ashamed of the way your Polish sounds. If your waiter/waitress understands you very well, you are successful.

Now it is time for something extra. Let's just chill out and stop memorizing phrases and vocabulary for a moment. Below is a list of traditional Polish meals that are definitely worth trying:

Kotlet schabowy – a breaded **pork** cutlet; made of **pork tenderloin** (with the bone or without), or a **pork chop**.

Pierogi – Polish dumplings; they come with different fillings (e.g., cheese, jam, fruits, meat, cabbage, mushrooms).

Bigos – very spicy stew based on **sauerkraut** and meat.

Gołąbki – cabbage leaves filled with spiced minced meat and rice.

Kiełbasa – a Polish sausage; yet it differs significantly from the English equivalent. It comes in different versions (e.g., fresh, smoked) and is made of different types of meat (pork, lamb, veal, game, beef, etc.).

Kapusta kiszona – sauerkraut.

Ogórek konserwowy – a pickled cucumber; rather sweet and vinegary in taste. **Sałatka warzywna (sałatka jarzynowa)** – vegetable salad; a traditional Polish side dish based on cooked vegetables (potato, carrot, parsley root, celery root) with eggs, pickled cucumbers, and mayonnaise.

Żurek – very traditional Polish sour rye soup; it contains eggs, Polish sausage, diced potatoes, diced carrots, meat, and mushrooms.

Pyry z gzikiem (Upper Poland) – potatoes (pyry) served with gzik (**quark** with **sour cream**, onion, and chives).

Bryndza (Lesser Poland) – sheep milk cheese.

Oscypek (Tatra Mountains) – hard, salty cheese from non-pasteurized **sheep's milk;** smoked over a fire and often served with some cranberry jam.

Cepeliny (Podlasie) – large and long potato dumplings filled with meat.

Kluski śląskie (Silesia) – round dumplings made of potatoes that are served with gravy.

These are the traditional dishes, yet there are many new Polish dishes worth trying. For example, if you are into street food, try *zapiekanka*—a short baguette topped with ham, mushrooms, tomato sauce, different vegetables, and mayonnaise. *Zapiekanka* comes in different varieties and sizes.

Apart from traditional cuisine, many restaurants offer food from all around the world (Italian, Chinese, Indian, etc.), so don't expect only restaurants that serve *pierogi* and *żurek*. Moreover, if you are on a plant-based diet, you will be surprised how many vegan restaurants can be found in Poland. In fact, Warsaw is in the top ten of European cities with the biggest amount of vegan and vegetarian restaurants.

Chapter 9 – Entertainment

A good trip consists of sightseeing and some entertainment. If you go on a trip on your own, it is up to you how you spend your time. Thus, keep in mind that Polish cities offer plenty of opportunities to enjoy in your free time. Moreover, the nightlife is amazing.

Cinema/Movies

Cinemas are quite popular in Poland. Cities such as Warsaw, Cracow or Poznan contain at least ten different cinemas, and some smaller cities offer at least one. The tickets usually are more expensive on weekends, so if you want to choose the cheapest way, go to the cinema on Wednesday or Thursday. Sometimes, tickets on weekends can cost twice as much! Below are some vocabulary and phrases that might be useful during your trip to the cinema:

Kino – cinema

Film – film/movie

Film akcji – action film

Thriller – thriller

Gatunek filmowy – a movie genre

Komedia romantyczna – romantic comedy

Komedia – comedy

Horror – horror film

Film historyczny – historical film

Film przygodowy – adventure film

Film science fiction – science-fiction film

Musical/film muzyczny – musical

Sala kinowa – screening room

Miejsce – seat

Rząd – row

Ekran – screen

Bar przekąskowy – snack bar

Popcorn – popcorn

Zimne napoje – cold beverages

Bilet do kina – cinema ticket

Now let's try a short exercise that will help you remember the words you have just learned.

Exercise: Say in Polish the following words.

seat

row

screen

snack bar

popcorn

cold beverages

cinema ticket

historical film

adventure film

science-fiction film

musical

cinema

film/movie

action film

thriller

a movie genre

romantic comedy

Before you go to the cinema, you have to, of course, choose your movie. We have prepared a short exercise that will allow you to discuss your favorite films with your friend. Remember the chapter in which we practiced likes/dislikes and like/love/hate phrases? It is time to use them again.

Exercise: There are a few situations. Using your previous knowledge and vocabulary from this chapter, try to discuss your favorite kind of film with your friend.

a) Tell your friend that you don't like romantic comedies.

b) Ask your friend what movie genre he/she likes the most.

c) Tell your friend that you love thrillers.

d) Tell your friend that you hate horror films.

Very good! You have chosen the film, so it is time to go to the cinema. Here are the most useful phrases:

Dzień dobry, poproszę dwa blilety. – Hello, two movie tickets, please.

Jaki film chciałby Pan/chciałaby Pani obejrzeć? – Which film would you like to see?

Chciałbym/chciałabym obejrzeć ten film. – I would like to see this film.

Proszę wybrać swoje miejsce. – Please, choose your seat.

Czy te dwa miejsca są wolne? – Are these two seats free?

Przykro mi, te miejsca nie są już wolne. – I'm sorry, these two are not available.

Czy mogę zabrać jedzenie i napoje na salę? – Can I take food and drink to the screening room?

Może Pan/Pani zabrać tylko jedzenie i picie zakupione w naszym barze. – You can take the food and beverages from our snack bar.

Przepraszam, gdzie jest bar z przekąskami? – Excuse me, where is the snack bar?

Dzień dobry, chciałbym/chciałabym kupić dwa duże popcorny. – Hello, I would like to buy two large popcorns.

Dobrze, czy coś do picia? – Okay, would you like something to drink?

Poproszę dwie duże cole. – Two large cokes, please.

Przepraszam, gdzie jest sala numer 8? – Excuse me, where is room number 8?

Prosimy o wyłączenie telefonów. – Please, switch off your phones.

Nagrywanie filmów jest zabronione. – Recording is not allowed.

Let's go through a short exercise.

Exercise: Try to choose the best Polish phrase.

    a) Buy two tickets.

    b) Ask the employee if these two seats are available.

    c) Order two large cokes.

    d) Ask the employee where room 8 is.

e) Ask the employee where the snack bar is.

f) Ask your friend which film he/she would like to see.

Excellent! You can go to the Polish cinema and order tickets in Polish.

At the Theater/Opera

Although theaters are not that popular when compared to previous decades, you can still enjoy some places that are worth visiting. Theaters in Poland can be found in cities such as Warsaw, Krakow, etc. Here is a list of the most important words connected to art:

Teatr – theater

Teatr muzyczny – musical theatre

Sztuka – play

Spektakl/przedstawienie – performance

Występować – perform

Aktor/aktorka – actor

Główna rola – lead/major role

Balet – ballet

Balet klasyczny – classical ballet

Kurtyna – curtain

Rekwizyt – prop/stage prop

Scena – stage

Opera – opera

Opera – opera house

Operetka – operetta

Musical – musical

Chór – choir

tancerz/tancerka – dancer

śpiewak operowy – opera singer (masculine)

śpiewaczka operowa – opera singer (feminine)

It is time to memorize the vocabulary through practice.

Exercise: Say the Polish equivalents of the English words below.

stage

opera

opera house

operetta

musical

choir

play

performance

perform

actor

ballet

classical ballet

curtain

prop/stage prop

Good! You are about to be ready to go to the Polish theater. Now imagine that you are sitting with your friend at a café and talking about art.

Exercise: Try to say it in Polish.

     a) Tell your friend that you love ballet.

     b) Tell your friend that you would like to see a play.

c) Tell your friend that you don't like the major role in the play.

d) Ask your friend if he/she likes ballet.

e) Ask your friend if he/she likes opera.

f) Tell your friend that you love musicals and ask if he/she does too.

Music and Nightlife

If you are in a different country, you definitely need to try the nightlife and get familiar with the music. There are plenty of nightclubs, pubs and good parties in each city in Poland. Moreover, parties do not finish at 2:00 am or 3:00 am, and Polish nightclubs are usually open till the early morning, so 6:00 am or even 7:00 am— yes, in Poland, you can party all night long! Apart from parties, many pubs offer live concerts, performances, and karaoke contests.

Let's learn some vocabulary connected to music:

Muzyka – music

Gatunek muzyczny – a music genre

Rock – rock music

Pop – pop music

Hip-hop – hip-hop

Muzyka taneczna – dance music

Koncert – a concert

Występ – a performance

Karaoke – karaoke

Płyta – an album

Utwór – a track

Piosenka – a song

Piosenkarz (male)/piosenkarka (fem.) – a singer

It is time to practice.

Exercise: Try to say these English sentences in Polish.

    a) Tell your friend that you like rock music.

    b) Ask your friend what music genre he/she likes the most.

    c) Tell your friend that you don't like pop music.

    d) Tell your friend that you love dance music.

Good! You can now discuss your favorite music.

Now, it is time to party:

Nocne życie – nightlife

Klub nocny/klub – nightclub

Klub muzyczny – music club

Bar/pub – bar/pub

Dyskoteka – disco

Barman – barman/bartender

Barmanka – barmaid/bartender

Parkiet – dance floor

Tańczyć – dance

Muzyka – music

Karaoke – karaoke

Śpiewać – sing

Imprezować – party

Spędzać czas z przyjaciółmi – spend time with friends

Zespół muzyczny – music group

DJ/didżej – DJ/club DJ

Drink/koktajl – cocktail

Loża VIP – VIP lounge

Ochroniarze – security guards

The words above are worth knowing if you want to party in Poland. Go through the list once again if you have forgotten most of the new words. If you haven't, let's practice.

Exercise: Say the Polish equivalents of the English words below.

music group

DJ/club DJ

cocktail

VIP lounge

security guards

music

karaoke

sing

party

nightlife

nightclub

music club

bar/pub

disco

barman/bartender

Excellent! You have learned a few words that might help you order your favorite drink or go to your favorite club. It is time to put these words in a real context by learning some useful phrases:

Cześć, chciałbym/chciałabym zamówić dwa koktajle. – Hi, I would like to buy two cocktails.

Oczywiście, jakie drinki? – Of course, which drinks?

Poproszę dwa z owocami. – I would like two drinks with some fruit.

Oczywiście. Czy mam dorzucić kostki lodu? – Of course. Would you like some ice cubes?

Tak, poproszę. – Yes, please.

Cześć, czy mogę prosić o kartę napojów? – Hi, can I have a cocktail menu?

Cześć, oto karta napojów. – Hi, here is the cocktail menu.

Przepraszam, o której startuje impreza? – Excuse me, what time does the party start?

Dobry wieczór, chciałbym/chciałabym zamówić lożę VIP dla 9 osób. – Hello, I would like to book a VIP lounge this night for nine people.

Oczywiście, to będzie 200 zł. – Of course, that will be 200 zł.

Exercise: Try to say the following in Polish.

> a) Order four cocktails and one beer.

> b) You don't know what time the party starts. Ask your friend.

> c) Book the VIP lounge.

> d) Ask the bartender to show you the cocktail menu.

Good job! Partying in Poland is no longer be a problem for you.

Short Revision

Let's sum up the whole entertainment chapter and get straight into practice.

Exercise: Try to say the following in Polish.

a) You are talking with your friend about movies. Tell him/her that you like romantic comedies, but you hate action films. Then, ask him/her what type of film he/she likes the most.

b) You are in a nightclub. Go to the bartender and order three drinks. Then go to the manager and book a VIP lounge for your friends.

c) You are in the cinema with your friend. Buy two tickets for the movie. Then go to the snack bar and buy two large popcorns and two large cokes.

d) You are talking with your friend about music. Tell him/her that you love pop music and rock music and that you hate dance music. Then ask him/her about his/her favorite music genre.

e) You are in the cinema. As your friend which film he/she would like to see.

f) Ask your friend if he/she likes ballet.

g) Ask your friend if he/she likes opera.

h) Tell your friend that you love ballet.

i) Tell your friend that you would like to see a play.

j) You don't know what time the party starts. Ask your friend.

Afterword

You have now faced an intensive language course and demanding exercises, but your language journey isn't over yet; this is just the beginning. This book should have been informative, educational, and provided a solid foundation of the Polish language. Now, being equipped with the basic knowledge, you are able and willing to continue your journey.

Remember that this book is not a one-time read. Every time you forget a word or a phrase, go back to whichever chapter you need. After all, systematic and consistent learning is all that counts. If you have the opportunity to go to Poland, don't hesitate—pack your things! Plus, a real, face-to-face conversation will teach you more than a hundred books ever could.

Let's summarize what you learned in this book:

      a) The basics of Polish—pronouns, verbs, nouns

      b) Grammatical background information

      c) The difference between formal and informal style

      d) Introducing yourself

      e) Counting to 100

      f) Discussing your likes/dislikes

g) Telling others about your mood and feelings

h) Telling others your telephone number, address, age, place of living, etc.

i) Doing shopping

j) Ordering a meal in a restaurant

k) Going to a nightclub/cinema/theater

l) Using Polish in an academic/school environment

m) Using Polish in a working environment

n) …and many more!

Getting to an advanced level requires self-discipline and dedication. Mastering a language is a tough and very long process, yet the result will always be rewarding. Good luck on your onward journey into the Polish language!

Finally, if you found this book useful in any way, a review on Amazon is always appreciated.